SUCCESSFUL STOCK MARKET

SPECULATION

(A Speculator's Manual)

T.E. Carter

Mistaya Publishing Ltd.
Cornwall, Ontario
Canada

Mistaya Publishing Ltd.
18108 Farlinger Drive, R.R.#1
Cornwall, Ontario
K6H 5R5
Phone: (613) 931-1175

Printed in Canada
First Printing, January 1991
Second Printing, October 1991
Third Printing, April 1992
Fourth Printing, April 1993
Fifth Printing, September 1993
Sixth Printing, February 1994
Seventh Printing, October 1996
Eighth Printing, April 1997
Ninth Printing, May 1999
Tenth Printing, September 2000

Canadian Cataloguing in Publication Data

Carter, T. E. (Thomas Edward), 1944-
Successful stock market speculation

Includes index.
ISBN 0-9695295-1-1

1. Speculation.   2. Stock-exchange.   I. Title.
HG6021.C37 1991   332.64'5   C91-091779-5

The publisher and the author do not guarantee or warrant that the readers who use the investment strategy in this book will achieve favorable results. Because of the speculative nature of some of the material in this book the publisher and author disclaim responsibility for any adverse consequences that might arise directly or indirectly from the use of such material.

For Gloria, without whom this project
would never have been completed.

Acknowledgements

THE AUTHOR wishes to thank Ed Vink for reviewing the manuscript and offering valuable suggestions and encouragement; Tom and Carol Berthelotte for their assistance in publishing and marketing; Gloria Croskery for typing the manuscript and giving encouragement; and Sally Clark for proofreading and showing me where the commas were supposed to go.

CONTENTS

Forward i
Introduction 3

Section I - The Warm-up
Your Investment Dollars 9
Who Plays the Market 12
The Market at Work 13
What is a Speculator? 15
Brokers 17
It's Time to Start 22

Section II - The Game
Think Like a Winner..27
System Evolution 28
Buying...32
Selling 36
Timing...37
Market Action 39
Risk 39
Pyramiding and Averaging Down 41
Market Letters and Analyst Reports 42
Bears and Bulls 43
Warrants and Rights 44
Cross Trading...46
Equipment Required 46
General Rules Before You Begin 47
General Thoughts...52

Section III - The Rules
How to Buy 57
    Market Action, Position and Depth 57
    Other Considerations 66
When to Sell 71
    Sell Indicators 74
Money Management 81
Buying Summary 87
Selling Summary 88
The Beginning 89
Appendix...93

FOREWORD

Anytime one writes a technical book, it is difficult to evaluate what topics should be discussed and what shouldn't. One has to have some feel about whom the readers will be. Since this book is about a very specialized area of market trading, i.e. stock speculation, I felt that the reader would already have some knowledge about the basics of trading in the market and should have some prior trading experience. Consequently, this book is not intended for someone who is investing for the first time.

Until one has experienced the volatility of the market firsthand (and this manual will definitely be dealing with some very volatile stocks), it is difficult to develop the proper attitude and discipline required to be a successful speculator, for speculation is definitely not for the faint of heart. Therefore, if you are a novice yet would like to use this system, I would suggest that you first read a book that will teach you the fundamentals of market trading. Secondly, talk to a good broker (ask your friends or business associates for recommendations). Thirdly, trade for awhile under the guidance of your broker. If you feel after doing all this you are prepared to accept the higher risks and faster pace intrinsic to speculating in the market, then put the ideas in this book to work for you.

Although this book is directed toward the speculator, it should be of interest to anyone who invests in the stock market. In particular, the rules in Section III in the segment on selling should be followed by anyone who owns stocks. Too often investors watch good stock picks go bad because they do not know when to sell.

This system was developed as a result of all the mistakes and successes I have experienced over a twenty-five year period of speculating in the stock market. There are no theories here, only rules by which to play the game. I have paid the price to learn these rules. I hope, through this book, that I can spare you many of the mistakes I have made and as a result, help you develop a consistent, winning investment strategy.

GOOD LUCK!

SUCCESSFUL STOCK MARKET

SPECULATION

(A Speculator's Manual)

INTRODUCTION

Investing in the stock market is intriguing for many people. This is evidenced by the fact that almost one quarter of all Canadians has money invested either in their own name or through mutual funds. It does not seem to matter what the market does, the attraction still remains. *Report on Business Magazine* (August 1990) states that, since the crash of October 19, 1987, almost 400,000 Canadians have invested in the market for the first time.

Most of these people trade their accounts on recommendations from outside sources such as brokers, friends, business associates, analyst reports, and trade journals. This is not surprising, as it would normally be a full time job trying to keep up with all that goes on in the market. This book will show you how to take direct control over at least one part of your stock portfolio - that part allocated to speculative issues.

I never purposely set out to develop a system for speculating in the stock market. It just naturally evolved through trial and error, mistakes and successes, and observation. I never realized I had actually created a successful strategy until 1983 when I discovered that I was both consciously and unconsciously following certain patterns and rules whenever I selected stocks to buy or sell. Although I considered putting my findings into a book at that time, I was busy starting up a new company and never gave it much more thought.

In 1986 I sold my interest in that company and semi-retired. The idea for a book began to crystallize then. I examined what I was doing in detail and broke the system down into its component parts. The result is the book you now have in your hands.

Many of you will already know some of the things contained in this book. I expect this because I didn't invent most of the concepts discussed here; they already existed. I have merely assimilated them into a practical system that is designed to give an easy to follow, step-by-step procedure for speculating in the stock market. Even though you may already be aware of many of these ideas and principles, no longer will they dance around in your head as unrelated, discrete pieces of information. They will be set into a unified structure that will enable you to develop an investment strategy that is both profitable and fun.

How often have you heard the expression, "Only people with inside information make any real money in the stock market," or something similar? It's true that some people are much better informed than others but whether they have actual "inside" information is debatable; some will and some won't. The real issue here is that there are people active in the market who are better informed than most. They do not get privileged information on every stock but on those they do they take action. For any given stock there will always be individual investors who have access to information much more quickly than "John Q. Public." These are the people who start market action. The procedures in this book are designed to try to identify that point when informed buying is taking place or, at the very least, determine when general buying interest has been generated in a stock and it is about to start or has just started a bull run.

Although informed buying usually will initiate a bull run on a stock, it is the psychology of the general buying public or uninformed buying that sustains it. When this type of buying dries up, it is important that you are no longer holding a position in that stock. This book will show you how to determine when you should sell.

To put it quite simply then, the system is a method that enables you to track the movements of both the informed and uninformed buying public. By tracking the actions of these people, you will know whether to buy or sell.

Knowing when to buy and sell stock is only part of successful speculation. It is also necessary to know how much of your financial resources should be allocated to any particular play. This most important aspect of speculating in the market is also dealt with in this book.

There is nothing magical about this system. To be successful with it you will have to devote time and effort. You will not be right every time you buy a stock. In fact, you will be wrong more often than you are right. It is the taking of proper action when you are right or wrong that will ensure your financial success.

By following the plan outlined in this book you will learn:
1) How to pick stocks.
2) When and how to buy and sell stocks.
3) How to manage your money within this framework.
4) How to maximize your return but minimize the amount of time spent.

Although the manner in which you will select stocks to buy will not be very conservative, you *will* be conservative in the way you handle your money. By combining these two elements, you will have a greater potential to make high returns with decreased risk.

Now I say to you, my friend, exercise diligence and discipline in committing this system to practice and I am sure financial success will follow. Once again,

GOOD LUCK!

SECTION I

THE WARM-UP

YOUR INVESTMENT DOLLARS

The primary intent of investing is to accumulate capital gains and increase wealth but secondarily, and just as importantly, it is also a means of preserving capital or wealth. Therefore, the minimum requirement of a successful investment is that its rate of return be large enough that any time in the future the spending power of the initial investment is maintained.

Anybody who earns more money than they spend is automatically an investor. Even the eccentric who keeps his money in a sock under the mattress or in a can buried in the backyard because he doesn't trust banks, is an investor because he is making an effort to preserve his capital against total loss because of bank failure or total economic collapse. It is unlikely that his investment has any growth potential but it definitely would in a period of deflation when his buying power would actually increase.

Most people spend almost no time monitoring their stock portfolios. Some may talk to their broker once a week or so (probably no more than half an hour per week), while others may talk to him only a few times a year. Yet they have thousands of hard-earned dollars invested. This is fine if one does not want to participate actively in one's financial growth, but is it smart? No! Remember, no-one has more interest in your financial future than you.

If you are truly concerned about your financial future, you should be prepared to invest some time as well as money on it. You have worked hard to earn the money you are investing and you therefore should not look lightly upon what is happening to it. I believe you should spend some

9

time every week monitoring your portfolio. How much is up to you, but I don't think an hour or two is unreasonable. If you feel you can't, or don't want to, take the time to manage your own hard-earned dollars then don't speculate. Buy some mutual funds that have good rates of return or have your broker recommend some good, dividend-paying, growth stocks.

Suppose you earn $50,000 annually. You probably work at least two thousand hours to earn this money. Now suppose you have $20,000 (which, by the way, took you over one thousand hours of work to accumulate after tax) invested in the stock market and you would like to make $10,000 with it in one year (which you have the potential to do by using the method described in this book). If you spend two thousand hours to earn $50,000, is it not logical that you should possibly spend four hundred hours to earn $10,000? This works out to approximately eight hours per week. Most people really cannot, or do not want to, spend this kind of time and therefore put their money in the hands of professionals, trusting they will do a good job. This book is for people who want to take a more active role in managing their financial future.

Once you become proficient at using the system in this book, you will likely spend no more than half an hour per day implementing it, i.e. the time you spend on coffee breaks or reading the newspaper in the morning. At first, however, you probably will spend about one hour a day, five days a week, until you improve your skills. If you can make fifty per cent or more on your money, it's not a bad way to spend your coffee-break, is it?

Each of us has different investment objectives and requirements. There are many factors, and combinations of these factors, which make each of our positions unique. Age, income, wealth, financial objectives, financial needs, marital status, number of dependents, career status, general life style, to name a few, all have a bearing on determining how our investment funds will be allocated. No matter what your personal position, a certain portion of your investment portfolio should be allocated to higher-risk/greater-return investments. There is no set rule determining what percentage of your portfolio should be in speculative issues but obviously a young person with his whole career ahead of him can take greater risks than a retiree who is dependent upon his investments for income.

There are many vehicles through which one's investment objectives can be realized (real estate, bonds, money markets, futures, etc.) and a good portfolio usually consists of a mix of these. Your particular mix will normally be determined by such factors as personal preference or expertise, attitude, aptitude, need and, yes, (it's not an obscene word) greed. This book is concerned with only one investment sector and that is the stock market - in particular that area of the market that can be considered speculative.

Unless you are a professional trader (in which case you are probably not reading this book), the money you commit to speculating in shares of publicly-traded corporations should be money that, if lost, will not seriously affect your financial well-being. By limiting your investment to only the amount you can afford to lose, you avoid the possibility (or probability) of being forced to trade prematurely. You will be able to play the game according to your dictates, not your bank account's. This does not mean that you shouldn't take winning the game seriously.

Previously I mentioned that there is no set rule determining what percentage of your investment portfolio should be of a speculative nature. This is true. I will, however, suggest that of the portion of your portfolio dedicated to stocks, you could easily allocate up to twenty percent to speculative issues if you are under forty years old, but you should use no more than five percent if you are a retiree. These are safety guide lines. If your temperament, attitude, aptitude and experience dictate that you can risk more, by all means go ahead, but accept the fact you may lose more than you can afford.

WHO PLAYS THE MARKET?

A survey conducted by the Toronto Stock Exchange shows that in 1989 twenty-three per cent of all Canadians owned stocks or mutual funds. This means that over 5.5 million Canadians invest in the stock market. Of these, well over 4 million own shares directly in their own name rather than through mutual funds. Further to this, as mentioned previously, since the market crash of October 1987, 400,000 Canadians have invested in the stock market for the first time. This suggests that the stock market is definitely a major attraction for investment funds and will likely continue to be, in spite of major setbacks such as the crash of 1987.

Although the rich and the super-rich can, and certainly do, exercise some control over the market and can most definitely have a direct influence on the performance of particular stocks, the market is still dominated, in terms of sheer numbers, by the smaller investor. Of the 4 million-plus Canadians who invest in the market only about eight per cent have accounts over $50,000 and most are less than $10,000 (*Report on Business Magazine*, August, 1990).

There is virtually no other place where a small investor can place his funds that is as easily accessible as the stock market. If one takes the time to manage these funds diligently and wisely, it also can be a place where fairly spectacular rates of return on investment can be achieved.

Most good mutual funds exhibit average rates of return between 10% - 18% annually, although in good years they have been known to have returns in the order of 25%. In general, though, most funds have 5 - 10 year rates of return between 7% - 10%. At the time of this writing many are losing money and most are struggling to show returns of even 4% - 5%. This situation has prevailed for several years. I believe that if you follow the method shown in this book and with a little luck, your rate of return will far and away outstrip any rates of returns that can be offered by mutual funds.

THE MARKET AT WORK

The stock market is an extremely dynamic investment vehicle, which is constantly in a state of flux. Market factors are continually at work creating changing investment environments for every stock or groups of stocks. Fundamental factors such as profit and loss statements, acts of God, new inventions, new fashions, new discoveries, interest rates, the economy in general, and others too numerous to mention, will all play a part in fixing market values. Since most of us don't have the time or the expertise to analyze when and how these factors are at work, we will leave that end of the market up to the professional analysts and traders. These people, very simply, have better information networks and personal connections than most of us have or can likely ever hope to have.

As important as fundamental factors may be in contributing to stock prices, securities are not priced solely on balance sheets and technical formulae. My experience indicates that the single most important factor affecting market movement and trends is investor psychology. No matter how compelling or powerful all the fundamental information may appear to be, if the investing public does not react to it, it means nothing. I have seen a small oil company drill an extremely successful oil or gas well and the stock did absolutely nothing, yet I've also seen a stock appreciate dramatically on just the potential that a successful well will be drilled. This is by no means the norm but it is the kind of occurrence that can make a fundamental analyst start looking for window ledges.

It is obvious that one must look beyond simple fundamental analysis to find what creates market dynamics and motivates investor psychology. This necessitates developing an approach that examines the effect of both fundamental and technical analysis on investor psychology. It is the observation and subsequent analysis of these effects that forms the substance of this book. Sections II and III explain in detail how to logically and methodically examine these effects and how to use this information to your advantage.

There is no greater indicator of how investors view a particular stock than the fluctuations in price and trading volume. Simple as this may sound, if one does not know how to assess the significance of these fluctuations, one cannot be a successful speculator. You will normally not be privy to the underlying reasons for a stock beginning to move because it would be impossible to track all stocks at all times. The changes could be due to professional trading, which then excites the interest of the general trading public; it could be the result of a favorable (or unfavorable) fundamental report done by an analyst who tracks that particular company; it could be due to a news release made by the company; promoter presentations to the securities industry on the value or prospects of the company may have motivated brokers to recommend the stock to their clients. Whatever the reason, changes in price and volume of a particular stock indicate if public interest has been piqued in that stock. This interest, by the way, can be negative as well as positive. The rules detailed in Section III will tell you whether sufficient interest has been generated to justify you buying this stock also.

There are always reasons for stock movement. Some may be fundamentally valid, some not. I am not too concerned with these reasons anymore. I am only interested in their effect on the market and in particular on specific stocks. It doesn't matter whether a market is bullish (stocks are generally on the rise) or bearish (stocks are declining) for, just as there are stocks that go down in bull markets, there are stocks that go up in bear markets. It is the development of the ability to pick those stocks that are going up out of the hundreds listed on the various stock exchanges that will make you a successful speculator. I will deal more specifically with all of the above material in Sections II and III.

WHAT IS A SPECULATOR?
Investor, speculator, player - all words that describe some-one who places some of his financial resources or capital

into the stock market for potential gain. When these words are heard, one automatically conjures up an image of the type of person to whom each would apply. My definitions may not agree with yours so I think it is appropriate that I discuss the terms as I shall use them.

a) Investor - implies one who invests capital for long-term growth at very low risk. His investment portfolio will usually be well-balanced in real estate, bonds, money markets, the stock market, etc. Of the money allocated to the stock market, most will be invested in blue chip or preferred stocks.

b) Player - one who dwells in the ozone of the speculative market. He is a high risk gambler. He will casually shoot money in small or large amounts for large potential gain as though he were playing craps. He has no organized game plan and will lay his money down on the slightest whim or a tip from his bartender or barber. His attitude is, "You win some, you lose some." Over the long term he usually loses.

c) Speculator - To me, the only thing a professional speculator has in common with the player is that they both take higher risks for higher potential gains. The similarity ends here. A legitimate speculator has a definite investment plan and goes about achieving it through a structured system. He knows how to widen the gap between risk and potential gain by decreasing his risk. Unlike the player, he never invests his money whimsically nor frivolously because he appreciates how hard it was to earn it in the first place.

BROKERS

As the securities industry has grown since the early days of Wall Street in New York and Bay Street in Toronto, the broker's function has become increasingly more complex. *Webster's Ninth New Collegiate Dictionary* defines broker as "one who acts as an intermediary: as an agent who negotiates contracts of purchase and sale (as of real estate, commodities, or securities)." You would be hard-pressed today to find a broker who would describe himself in such simple terms. Most have come to see themselves first as financial advisers who make recommendations to their clients on what investments to make and secondly as individuals who execute trades when a client wants to buy or sell those investments. There are others who assume the role of money manager for their clients and others see themselves as the "great deal" makers. None would describe themselves as just order takers. Unfortunately, this transition from order executor to financial manager occurred much more rapidly than did the sophistication or the education of the industry as a whole. Many brokers were ill-qualified to assume the stature of financial manager either through lack of experience (40% of all stock brokers have less than four years' experience), lack of education or a combination of both. Fortunately, the brokerage industry has recognized this and is now trying to rectify the problem through better hiring practices. Today you will see more lawyers, accountants, and MBA's in the business than ever before. In fact, the brokerage industry boasts that three out of four brokers now have some university education (*Report on Business Magazine*, August 1990).

The securities industry, through a need and a desire to

develop a more professional and sophisticated public image, allowed the investing public themselves to contribute to the development of this perception of their role as money managers and financial planners. In the past, professional financial management consultants were only available to the more wealthy investor and their fees were prohibitive for the smaller client. (This situation, in no small way, opened the door for mutual funds to develop a market niche.) As a result, the smaller client who required such services, allowed the mantle to be assumed by his broker, thinking that the broker at least knew more about investments than he did. So the broker's role evolved to what it is today. The industry now has a responsibility to ensure that its brokers are capable of wearing this mantle.

When a wealthy investor places funds with a professional money manager he can normally be confident that his and the money manager's objectives are not in conflict. The money manager agrees for a specified fee or contractual arrangement to invest his client's money to the best of his ability. If he does well, the relationship will usually continue. If he does not, he will be looking for a new client. The arrangement is not so simple for the poor stock broker. He must serve two masters - his company and his client, and their respective objectives may have no resemblance to each other whatsoever.

A large part of most brokerage houses' business comes from underwriting stock issues. Consequently a large part of the broker's job is to sell these issues to the public. This can result in a client being pressured into buying stocks he neither wants nor needs. It also can result in a broker having to sell a product he does not really believe in. The brokerage firm may think (for whatever reasons) that an issue has merit and therefore does a full underwriting. A broker may have his own reasons for not being as bullish about the issue as his company, yet, as an employee of the firm, he is required to sell it. If the company is right in its evaluation and the stock performs well, he looks good to his clients, if not, he may be looking for new clients.

Sometimes a brokerage firm does not think a particular new issue is solid enough to do a full underwriting and will agree to sell it to the public on a "best efforts" basis. Now the broker is faced with selling a product to his clients that even his own company is not prepared to underwrite fully. I am not against this practice, for it is a greatly needed service for start-up public companies. I am merely trying to point out the conflicts that can arise between a broker, his client and his company. Although the various provincial securities commissions have instituted rules requiring brokers to "know their clients," over the years I have encountered many who just want another name when it comes to selling new issues.

A third area of conflict originates because a broker makes his money through commissions. (It should be noted that some brokerage firms are introducing annual fee-based accounts but to date this service is available only to clients with large accounts.) He makes money when a client buys or sells a stock. An unscrupulous broker can increase his income by using high pressure tactics to get his clients to trade frequently. Fortunately this kind of broker will eventually be weeded out of the business. However, over the short term, he can go a long way towards destroying investor confidence, especially if he has had many dealings with beginners. Even the most honorable of brokers may be tempted to induce client trading if his commissions begin to dwindle. I think we are dealing mostly with an ethical issue here as ultimately the client is responsible for his own actions, regardless of any pressure placed on him to trade. If you are uncomfortable with the selling practices of your broker, find another but let your former broker know why you are taking your business elsewhere. He may become a better broker for it.

I will now describe the kind of broker you will need if you are going to follow the system in this book. First, and foremost, he must execute orders without question. If you say "buy," he buys and if you say "sell," he sells. He offers no unsolicited opinions or advice. In fact, if he does and does so frequently, you probably should be looking for a new broker. Secondly, he must be able to get information for you quickly when required. The kind of information you may need to know from him will be discussed in Sections II and III. That's it. Make sure he understands these simple parameters fully when you start dealing with him and hopefully you will have a long and prosperous relationship. Remember, he must execute trades and offer no unsolicited advice, i.e. "Don't call me I'll call you." I would also recommend that he not be a friend or a relative. Keep your business with him friendly but professional. Your judgement can be too easily clouded if you are too close to him.

You may ask, "If the guidelines are so simple, why not just use a discount broker?" My answer is, "You can." If you know exactly what trade you want to make and require no other information, by all means make your transaction with a discount house. Keep in mind, however, that a discount house is not always the cheapest place to trade. Furthermore, commission rates can vary substantially between the individual firms within the discount trading industry. The more expensive firms usually offer additional services such as twenty-four hour telephone ordering and free access to current market quotes. You should shop around for the firm that best suits your trading style and needs.

Discount brokers have a commission schedule that is typically comprised of a flat fee of $25 - $40 plus a charge ranging from 1/2 cent to 7 cents per share depending upon the price of the shares traded. For transactions less than $2000 a flat fee of $25 - $45 is charged depending upon which broker you use.

A full-service broker will charge commissions on a graduated scale up to 3.75% - 4% depending on the price of the stock and the value of the trade. Minimum commissions are normally in the $60 - $85 range.

I maintain accounts with both types of brokerage firms. Because I use a computer with software that allows me to access the information I need to make most of my trading decisions, I don't really need to trade with a full-service firm. This is not the case, however. By trading reasonably frequently with my full-service broker, I am able to obtain reports generated by his research department and also take advantage of turn-around commissions.

If you are a frequent trader, you should be able to negotiate turn-around commissions with your broker. This enables you to pay full commission when you buy a stock but only half commission when you sell. This can result in a lower commission than you would have paid at a discount broker. Depending on the overall volume and value of your trades you may be able to negotiate slightly lower commission rates as well. You should note that, for heavy traders, some discount brokers offer rebates of five per cent if commissions exceed $500 in a given quarter and ten per cent if they exceed $1000.

For those of you who do not have a computer and will be relying exclusively on a full-service broker for some of the information required to follow this system, don't use him for information and then go rushing off to a discount house. He will soon tire of you and you will lose a valuable and extremely helpful contact. Don't be afraid to ask him for a better deal on commissions, however.

For those who will be using computers to obtain information, open an account at a full-service firm as I have. Whenever you use your broker to obtain information about a stock for you, however, have the courtesy to give him the trade. Remember, sometimes you can trade with him just as cheaply as you can with a discount house if you negotiate commissions.

IT'S TIME TO START

In the next two sections you will see how the system grew out of observable market indicators and learn very specific rules about how you can make these indicators work for you. I developed these rules over a period of twenty-five years and use them myself daily. Because of my familiarity with them, some are mentally grouped together for me and it takes me very little time to apply them. When you start you should take them one step at a time until you are fully familiar with them. I have tried to put the rules in a logical order so that the groupings will come naturally to you when you start taking short-cuts. It takes me less than half an hour a day to use this system and I'm sure, with practice, you will reach this level too.

Experience is the best teacher when playing the market. Only through actual trading will you learn and profit from your mistakes and develop better instincts about the market. This book is only the start. Like a good athlete, even natural skills require practice to reach full potential and, with practice, the game becomes easier to play.

Whenever I have broken the rules in this book, I have found it has usually cost me money. Therefore, I say to you, develop DISCIPLINE, my friend, for without it you cannot succeed. I continually have to fight to maintain discipline even after twenty-five years and still I go astray from time to time. The only time I win consistently is when I follow the rules religiously. I know it will be hard but it is well worth the effort.

DISCIPLINE !!!

SECTION II

THE GAME

THINK LIKE A WINNER

Speculating in the stock market can be looked upon as a game. There are winners and losers. Special skills are required. There are rules that should be followed and best of all, it can be fun. Of course, most of the fun comes from winning. The goal of this book is to teach you the rules and how to develop the skills required to become a winner and thereby have a lot of fun while making money consistently.

As with any game or sport, no team or player wins 100% of the time and you should not expect to do so in this game. All great championship teams and champion players, however, ultimately win overall, in spite of any setbacks or losses they may incur. It is this ability to bounce back from adversity, coupled with superior skills that makes them great.

There are many highly skilled and talented teams and athletes who never become champions. What makes them different? I believe one of the big factors is how they deal with failure. Successful teams use failure to learn and develop winning strategies and attitudes. They do not dwell upon their mistakes and failures any longer than it takes to learn from them. They then move on and more finely tune their talents and skills using the things they have learned to ultimately develop championship form.

I do not mean to imply that we only learn through failure for champions certainly learn from their successes also, but successes never show you your weaknesses; only failure can do this. It is the recognition and strengthening of areas in which one is weak that helps prevent the reoccurrence of failure and makes one a more consistent winner.

27

It is not good enough merely to know about one's weaknesses and strengths. As all athletes know, training and practice are required to achieve excellence or championship form. The same commitment to practice and training is required to be successful in stock market speculation. Only through actual trading and having successes and failures, can your skills and mental attitude be truly honed to championship caliber. You will play the game less efficiently and make more mistakes at the start but you will get increasingly more proficient as time goes on, just as an athlete does. Eventually you will develop championship form and a winning attitude.

I was in the Oklahoma Sooners' clubhouse at the University of Oklahoma one time and there, written above the door to the playing field, were the great coach Bud Wilkinson's words, "Think like winners today." It is not enough to develop only your physical skills. You also must develop that winning attitude. You must be mentally prepared to handle all aspects of the game. Deal with both your successes and failures like a winner.

SYSTEM EVOLUTION

Like most of you, in my early years, I too bought most of my stocks on the recommendations of others. After a time, I began to notice there appeared to be a cyclical nature to the price and volume movement of some stocks, especially penny mining stocks. I found these movements, in the case of the mining stocks, generally coincided with exploration seasons and the public release of information about the results of such exploration. There were other factors involved as well, but they did not seem to carry the same weight.

This accounted for the mining stocks, but what about the others? My curiosity led me into the area of stock charting. By this time, my touting friends and brokers were having less than spectacular success (in fact they were downright dismal) in recommending stocks to me. I decided that if I were to continue to invest in the market, I must learn to do something for myself. So off to the library I went and found some information on how to chart and analyze stocks.

Over the next year I diligently charted and analyzed a selected group of stocks. By the end of the year, I had made no money. Why not? First, there are so many publicly traded companies it is impossible to chart them all. Therefore I was relying on a great deal of luck in selecting those stocks I would chart. There were some chart services available but, at the time, I felt I could not afford them. Even if I had subscribed to a service, not all stocks were charted anyway and furthermore, I would not have had the time to look at all the ones that were. Secondly, and most importantly, even if a stock exhibits an ideal chart there is no guarantee that its price will go up. There are more factors at work than just price and volume movements. Thirdly, when a chart shows that a breakout point has been reached, you need other information to decide whether the breakout will be up or down. Most of the time I did not have access to this additional information.

That year was not wasted however. It showed me that there is a definite place for technical tracking and analysis in investment strategy but it is only one part of the whole picture. I believe that one who makes his investments solely through charting will eventually lose money in the long run. This is just a feeling; I have no data or statistics to back it up.

Because I realized charting was only a tool to be used along with other market information for making my investment decisions, it led me to develop a short-cut method of obtaining and using the more important elements of charts without having to actually create the charts or analyze them. This method also allows me to monitor all stocks. How this is done will be shown in Section III.

I now had the technical part of the system developed but I still had to determine what other factors were at work while only having a limited amount of information available to me. While puzzling over this dilemma I decided to propose a theory and then see if information was readily available that would enable me to put it into practice. This is it:

The market itself can tell you what is going on.

After years of study and observation, I eventually pieced together a correlation between information that can be gathered on a daily or weekly basis from newspaper stock listings and what action should be taken as a result of this information. I found that if proper action was taken according to a specified set of rules and investment funds were properly managed within the framework of these rules, one could speculate successfully and make high rates of return at a much lower risk.

The key elements of the system are:

    1) Market Action
    2) Stock Position
    3) Market Depth
    4) Money Management

There are other elements that will be considered but they are of lesser importance and will be discussed later.

I found that by using these key elements it was no longer necessary to know the underlying causes of a stock's movement. The fact that it was moving and met all the parameters of the system was enough. If I was in error in buying a stock as a result of the first three key elements, the fourth prevented any real disasters from occurring. I also began to find that, because it was unnecessary to know the underlying causes of a stock's movement, too much information about a stock could be detrimental as this information could entice me to break the rules. I would become more concerned with other factors rather than the fact that the stock was moving up.

A good example of this is buying a gold stock when the price of gold is going down. I would get more concerned about the price of gold, which was irrelevant because the price of the stock was going up. There had to be other factors pushing the stock up that I knew nothing about. Yet every day the price of gold would affect my view of the stock.

Earlier I mentioned that, above all things, discipline is required in order not to break the rules (they may be stretched as you will see later). In closing this section I would like to tell you a story.

I had been out nightclubbing one night and got home about 2:30AM. I had a good glow on and was not tired so I poured myself a nightcap and sat there thinking about my dealings with a particular broker I was using at the time. Every stock in my account with him had been bought on his recommendation and it was a disaster. By this time I had developed the system to the point where I knew how to select stocks to buy but I hadn't given much consideration to how and when to sell.

I sat there for a while brooding over all the losers in that account and began to get angry. I knew that he arrived at the office every morning at about 6:30 so I sat up and waited. At 6:35 I phoned him and told him to sell everything in my account and I would call him before 8:00 to tell him what to buy.

As luck would have it, that day there was a stock listed in the paper that fit all my buying parameters exactly. I called him back and told him to buy 1000 shares at $16 and to sell at $19.50. I was going to show him how to play the market properly. I then went to sleep. The next day he called me and said, "I've got some good news and some bad news. The good news is you bought at $16 and sold at $19.50. The bad news is it opened at $22 this morning." That stock went to over $30.

I was pragmatic about this. After all, I had just made $3500 in one day (less commissions of course). But of even more importance, I learned how emotion and lack of discipline can cloud one's judgement and cost money. I am not saying I would have held the stock until it peaked, but I may have held it until it reached the high twenties if I had known what factors to look for that would enable me to determine when it is time to sell.

BUYING

In Section III you will find rules and guidelines that show you how to pick specific stocks to buy. Before you start learning how to buy in detail, I think some general comments on buying will be helpful.

When you put what you learn from this book into practice, you will only buy issues that you have selected yourself. It is always better to buy something than be sold something. When you buy, all the reasons for buying should be your own but when you are sold something, you are buying because someone else wants you to buy. Often your own convictions may be compromised by a good sales presentation. Good professional salespersons know how to sell you things you do not really want or need. They know how to pull your strings. One of the main objectives of this book is to teach you how to make your own selections. You will, therefore, make all efforts to resist buying stocks you have not selected yourself.

Selecting stocks yourself does not mean that you will ignore recommendations from other sources. When your broker or a stock analyst suggests that particular stocks are possibly good buys, they probably have some valid reasons for doing so. You should take these recommendations under advisement and monitor their performance. Only when (or if) they fall within your parameters for buying will you establish a position, not before. The decision to buy still remains in your control.

The only issues you will buy will be seasoned, actively traded, listed stocks. You will not buy initial public offerings (IPOs), secondary distributions or special offerings. It is very difficult to assess whether IPOs or new issues are priced right for the market. This can only be determined once they begin trading. These stocks could be overpriced because the cost of issuing them is built into the selling price. Because much thought and effort has gone into establishing what is the best price for the issue, most times there will not be much room for any great potential capital gain. Although the securities industry is rife with stories of new issues that have come on the market at $0.50 and gone to $5.00 or $10.00, these occurrences are so rare they are not worth the risk of buying. If a stock was worth $10.00 in the first place, why was it issued at $0.50? Many times the gains made are only a result of promotion and hype, not real value.

When you see some of these low-priced stocks start to escalate dramatically in value, it is sometimes wise to look at the company's total market capitalization. Multiply the total number of shares outstanding by the price per share and see what value the public is placing on the company. The results can sometimes be quite scary. You may find a company with a market capitalization of $2,000,000 yet its only asset may be an unproven mining claim that it paid $200,000 for.

Although we all have the innate desire to buy at the low and sell at the high, in reality, this is not what makes a successful speculator. For sure, he buys lower and sells higher - in fact, you will be looking to buy stocks with the potential to double in value - but he does not attempt to determine when a stock has hit its low. In other words he is not a bargain hunter. Instead, he searches for stocks that are already moving up and exhibit indications that they will continue to do so for some time. He wants to buy stocks that show good strength in price and volume and have a broad buying interest. When a stock begins to show signs that the bull run is over, he sells. It does not matter that the stock may gain a little more after he sells. Thus, he is usually trading in some range between the stock's low and high. He does not try to identify these points. You will learn to trade in this manner in Section III.

The two key factors in buying any stock is that its price is rising on strength and it is liquid. Stocks on the rise can often stimulate additional buying because they become noticeable to other investors. As a matter of fact your own buying, using the system in this book, will be partially initiated through current buying.

The importance of liquidity should be obvious. There is no point in buying a stock that will be hard to sell when it comes time to do so. Generally, a stock that is hard to buy (you usually have to pay a premium to buy it) and easy to sell, will be a stock that is on the rise.

Most of the stocks you will buy will be for the short term, i.e. days, weeks or months. It may turn out that because of exceptional performance, you will find yourself holding a stock for a much longer period, but this will be rare. Short term investing holds more attraction for me than settling in for the long haul because I think it is much easier to see what lies just ahead than what will occur a year or two from now.

Don't get disillusioned when you start out buying losers. If I knew how to be right 100% of the time and told you how to do it, everybody would buy this book. Eventually they would all want to quit their jobs and only play the market. This would leave no labour force for the companies traded on the stock exchange. They would go broke. Their stock would collapse and everything I told you would then be wrong.

It is inevitable that you will be wrong more than you are right. By following the rules in Section III, however, the times you are right should more than compensate for the times you are wrong. Perseverance and discipline will eventually pay off.

The object of this book is to show you how you can potentially double your investment funds annually. In attempting to do this you should, at the very least, make returns that are unavailable to you through most other investment mediums. If you already have a million dollars, a ten per cent return is quite attractive. Most of us can be quite comfortable on an income of $100,000 per year. If you only have $5000 to invest, ten per cent is not going to make you rich very quickly. Yes, I know all about the effects of compound interest but ten per cent is not a rate of return that I find to be very attractive. At this rate your money doubles in just over seven years. But if you can make twenty, thirty or one hundred per cent on this money, it's possible to double your money in three years or less.

SELLING

The first rule of selling is that you never sell a stock without a good reason for doing so. Do not get rid of a winner just because the opportunity arises to buy another stock that fits this system. The stock that is already a winner is the one you should continue to hold until market indicators dictate that you should sell. This does not mean that once you are fully invested you no longer scan the stock pages for new opportunities. The time is going to come when some winners must be sold because of decreasing performance and you should be prepared to move into other potential winners. Furthermore, the more often you scan the stock listings the more familiar you will become with the performance of individual issues.

The second simple rule of selling is never hold onto your losers. Sticking with a loser usually incurs a double penalty: it continues to decline; it ties up funds that could be used to buy a stock that is advancing. You have no control over getting the price of the stock back up but by selling you can prevent any further erosion of your capital. You can then take the remainder of your money and buy a stock that is on the move.

Before you begin using this system, you will sell all the deadwood in your account. Even if you will be taking large losses on some issues it is time to put your money back to work. This is your first test of discipline. If you can't sell these losers you probably will not be able to follow this system.

TIMING

Timing is the key element in any purchase or sale. You will develop a better sense of timing with experience but until then here are a few tips that may help you.

To gain experience and develop timing you must trade. Whenever you make a purchase and it does not perform well, sell it and look for something better. There is no point in holding onto stocks that are sitting in the doldrums if there are other stocks available that are moving up. Even if no better stocks are available at a given time it is better to be out of the market altogether than holding non-performers - at least your cash can earn interest and is readily available when a good prospect presents itself.

Often you will buy stocks where all indications are that it is ready to move but it does not. It is possible your timing is wrong and you should not wait around for something to happen. Sell your position and wait for a better opportunity to come along. If, at a later date, that particular stock begins to perform you can always buy it again, even if it means paying more than what you sold for.

There are times when certain stocks are out of sync with the general market. Timing plays a key role here. For example, if after a long bull market a stock begins to show strength, this is probably a bad sign because it took too long to react to good conditions but if a stock takes a long time to react to a bear market this could be a good sign. A stock that goes down much more slowly than other stocks in a bear market may advance much more quickly when the bull begins to run. These stocks could also be a precursor of a market turn-around. If they begin to show price and volume strength during a bear market perhaps the bull is just around the corner. Conversely, that stock that took so long to react to the bull market could be a precursor of a bear coming through the door. It could indicate that the market is so overbought that the buying public has even become interested in the weak sisters.

Although timing is important when you buy a stock I think it is even more so when you decide to sell. Basically when you look at a buying opportunity one of three things occurs - you decide not to buy and the worst that can happen is you miss an opportunity; you buy and are wrong, which will not be disastrous because you will sell the stock quickly and cut your losses; you will buy and the stock performs well. To be successful you must make the most out of your good performers because these are the stocks that will compensate for your wrong decisions. Section III outlines the things to look for to determine whether or not it is time to sell. As long as a stock continues to rise on large trading volumes you can feel confident in continuing to hold but once danger signals rear their head, take appropriate action.

MARKET ACTION

By the time you finish reading this book you probably will be sick and tired of hearing this statement but here it is again. There are no indicators of what the market is doing that are as important as price and volume movement. It does not matter what your broker says or what analysts recommend or what the underlying fundamental strengths of a stock may be, they are worth exactly what you can buy or sell them for; nothing more, nothing less. Until the buying public perceives the stock to have some merit and begins buying, the stock will not likely move. The recommendations of the brokers and analysts can definitely incite buying but until the stock actually begins to react there is no point in buying it. Too often have I seen glowing reports on companies and the stocks have made no significant moves, or worse, they have actually gone down. It is not worth the risk of trying to outguess the market without good reason; let it tell you when it is ready.

RISK

Speculation is the art of taking higher risks for higher returns. Successful speculators know how to decrease the risk yet still get higher returns.

The only factor over which you have absolute control when you invest in the market is your degree of risk. It can never be eliminated -only reduced.

Normally as risk is decreased so is the potential rate of return. Even the most conservative of portfolios contains a certain degree of risk because no one can predict the future with one hundred per cent accuracy. Conservative portfolios, however, usually have lower rates of return. Even so, one day's blue chip can be another day's dog.

The first way to decrease your risk is to limit the amount of money you could possibly lose in any given venture. This is done in two ways:

1) Only commit a fixed percentage of your total funds to the purchase of any one issue.

2) Cut your losses if you have chosen badly, i.e. set a limit as to how far a stock can drop before you sell.

How to set these percentages and limits is discussed in detail in Section III.

The second way to decrease your risk is to only buy stocks that appear to be positioned for large potential advances yet have a low downside risk. This is achieved by buying at the right price at the right time. Never buy a stock where the downside potential is greater than its potential gain. Again, how to do this is discussed in Section III.

It is this combination of good money management and astute stock selection that will decrease your risk yet yield high returns. The prime objective here is to earn capital gains. If it turns out that you pick a stock that pays dividends as well, this is a bonus. Even if all you buy are blue chip stocks, you have to realize capital gains if you are to make any kind of respectable rate of return. Strangely enough many people invest in these stocks as income producing investments when they would be better off just putting their money in the bank because with many so-called blue chip stocks their chances of making any reasonable capital gain are virtually nil. Yet these people feel they are investors not speculators.

PYRAMIDING AND AVERAGING DOWN

NEVER, NEVER average down.

Averaging down is the process by which a person buys a stock and then begins to accumulate more if the price begins to drop. The rationale behind this action is that the average price at which the stock is purchased is decreased. It is expected that once the stock bottoms out and begins to recover, it does not have to rise as much before a profit can be made or the original investment is recovered. The biggest drawback to this is that, more often than not, the stock never recovers and as the price continues to drop, the rate at which money is lost increases in direct proportion to the number of additional shares purchased. I say, once again, cut your losses and put the remaining funds into a stock that is going up instead of buying more of a stock that is going down. If you average down you could wait forever for the stock to recover and thus your money just lies idle.

Averaging down was a popular theory many years ago because so-called "experts" said that over the long term the general trend of the stock market was up. Although this may be true, in order to take advantage of it you would have to purchase a broad cross-section of stocks in all industries. Even then your gains would be marginal. I don't believe it

41

was ever intended to apply to individual stocks but it would appear that a little knowledge is a dangerous thing, for that is exactly what inexperienced investors began doing. There is never any guarantee that an individual stock will ever recover ground it has lost. It is possible the stock may even drop off the board altogether.

Pyramiding is the opposite of averaging down. As a stock begins to become stronger and stronger and the price increases, more stock is bought. People who pyramid normally do so because they were unsure of the stock's potential when they first bought so they took a small position. Once the stock began to show exceptional strength they wanted a larger position. Pyramiding is especially popular when stocks are making new highs, because, as these new highs continue to be reached, the average purchase price can be much lower if the stock has been accumulated at regular intervals on the way up.

When you follow the system in this book, the only time you will ever pyramid is when you did not get your desired position filled when you first bought the stock. Once you have achieved this goal (either through obtaining the number of shares you wanted initially or through spending your dollar investment limit) you will stop buying. Hopefully, pyramiding will be a rarity as you will be able to fill your requirements when you first purchase.

MARKET LETTERS AND ANALYST REPORTS

For clarity's sake, I differentiate between Market Letters and Analyst Reports. Market Letters are those that you pay an annual fee to subscribe to, whereas Analyst Reports are created in-house by the various brokerage firms. Most brokerage houses have different areas of expertise and thus their reports are slanted more toward these areas. It is important to know the strength of a particular house when reading its reports.

I have subscribed to Hume Publishing's *Moneyletter* and also receive reports from the various houses with which I have accounts. Some of these reports are excellent. I do not, however, buy stocks on their recommendations. I read these reports out of general interest and monitor their recommendations for they could create some buying interest. If any of their stock picks begin to perform according to the parameters in this book, I buy them without hesitation for there is usually some substance behind these stocks.

BEARS AND BULLS

A bear market is one in which the general trend of stock prices is down and in a bull market the trend is up. In a bear market there are stocks that go up, just as in a bull market there are stocks that go down. In either market there can be brief periods of recovery (in a bear) or decline (in a bull). In a bull market a stock that reacts the least to a decline will usually advance more quickly and further when the bull resumes its run. When a bear market starts, some stocks that appear to be withstanding the general downward pressure may only be postponing the inevitable. After a bear is in full swing, however, stocks showing extraordinary strength should be looked at seriously.

In a bull market you will find many stocks that fit the parameters of this book daily. You can't buy them all, so you must select the ones that show exceptional performance and strength. These are the stocks that have the best combination of price advance, trading volume and broad buying interest.

In a bear market, very few issues will fit the parameters so there is much less work to do. Many days you will find no stocks at all. If the bear market has been fairly prolonged it will inevitably break. Before this occurs there will be some stocks that begin to show exceptional strength. These stocks likely will become market leaders when the bull begins.

Even though very few stocks present themselves as potential investments in a bear market you can still profit from buying those that do. Some stocks even make new highs during a bear but normally you can expect lower rates of gain.

For brief periods of time during either bull or bear markets some groups of stocks will buck the trends. This is usually because of particular economic or political factors that create a different climate for those particular industries. A good example of this was the political situation during the war in Iraq. The price of oil soared as well as the quarterly earnings of many oil companies. The effect of those earnings and prices never really filtered through to the price of the oil stocks, but if the situation had continued or worsened, it would have been inevitable. As it turned out the high prices of oil were short-lived, which also shows how emotional and reactive investors can be.

WARRANTS AND RIGHTS

Some companies have issued warrants or rights that allow holders to purchase stock at some future date at a fixed price. Usually these were issued in conjunction with some investment package that included a combination of common stock and warrants or rights. These securities are normally traded just like common stock. If the price of the stock goes up, the warrants will follow along with it.

If a stock looks bullish, buying warrants is an inexpensive way of taking advantage of the stock's gain. There will usually be a premium paid for buying these warrants but if the potential for profit is great, the premium will not matter.

Suppose that a warrant is issued that allows the holder to buy stock in a company for $3.00 per share prior to a specified expiry date. The stock then moves to $5.00 per share. The warrant would likely be trading around $2.50. This means, should you exercise your right to buy stock at $3.00, it would cost you $5.50 per share ($2.50 + $3.00). If the stock continued to rise to perhaps $10.00 per share, the warrant would probably advance to $7.50. Therefore, on the warrant you would have tripled your investment but only doubled it if you had bought common stock.

Four things should be considered when buying warrants or rights. First, of course, is your evaluation of how high the stock itself is likely to go. Second, what premium on price are you paying? If it is perceived that the stock is going to be strong, the premium will be high. You must think the stock will go high enough to surpass the combined cost of the warrant plus the exercise price before you buy. Thus, the third thing you must find out is the exercise price. Your broker can find this out for you. The last thing you need to know is the expiry date. Your broker can tell you this date. If the expiry date is imminent you should not buy. You need to have a long enough time for the stock to appreciate after you buy the warrant. Usually as the warrant's expiry date approaches, the premium you pay will begin to drop.

CROSS TRADING

There is an accepted practice in the stock market where stock trades can be made without going through the exchange floor. This can occur when a broker has both a buyer and a seller on his own book and he expedites the trade himself, or two brokers within the same house execute a trade when one has a buyer and the other has a seller. This can even take place between two brokers in different houses.

There are mixed feelings about this practice as it can leave room for stock manipulation or other unethical practices. However, it does allow large trades to take place without seriously affecting the market.

The general rule is that the trade must take place at a level either at the bid price, the offer, or somewhere in between. My own feeling is that if there is a bid or offer on the floor of the exchange at the price a cross is going to be transacted, it should be filled first. Many times an investor reads the stock listings and sees large (or small) volumes trade at his desired price yet his order goes unfilled. This explains why this sometimes happens.

EQUIPMENT REQUIRED

As in any game you will require specific equipment to speculate in the stock market. You already have acquired your first piece by buying this book. Next you will need a subscription to either *The Globe and Mail* or *The Financial Post*. Most local daily newspapers do not give complete enough stock listings to obtain all the information you will need to use this system effectively. Third, buy some columnar pads (see examples in the appendix) or if you have a computer set up a spread sheet file so that you can analyze and monitor your daily work and keep track of all your purchases and sales. It is absolutely imperative that you record all the information about a stock that is necessary to follow this system assiduously. Fourth, you will need a stockbroker who understands your goals and objectives and has the ability to help fulfill your objectives effectively. More will be said on brokers later.

Once you have all this equipment in place you are ready to begin.

GENERAL RULES BEFORE YOU BEGIN

Before you begin trading I am going to outline some restrictive rules, some of which you are free to change only after you have gained enough trading experience that you are confident your instincts and attitude have developed to the point that you can become more aggressive.

    1) Only Trade TSE - There are enough stocks listed on the Toronto Stock Exchange so that, at the start, you will have no need to look elsewhere. Although some of the listed companies have fallen on hard times over the years, the TSE still has somewhat substantial listing requirements. You therefore will have a better chance of picking a more stable company than on Canada's other three exchanges. If *The Globe and Mail* is your newspaper of choice, you will find that it does not publish enough information about the other exchanges on a daily basis for you to follow this system in any event.

Being the largest stock exchange in Canada, the TSE also attracts more buying and selling. Since you only want to be trading in active, listed stocks this is an additional benefit. I still do most of my trading on the TSE.

When you decide it's time to start trading on other exchanges, I recommend the Vancouver Stock Exchange. For sheer fun and excitement there is nothing like it. Some very good resource companies now trading on the TSE had their beginnings on the VSE.

The VSE in the past has had its problems due to shady promoters and trading practices but they are making an effort to clean up their act. I still think it is much riskier trading there but I enjoy the action. If you begin trading on this exchange you will require a subscription to *The Financial Post* as *The Globe and Mail* does not print enough information on a daily basis.

I never trade on the Alberta Stock Exchange, primarily because there is not enough information published regularly. You can get the information you require from your broker, but this is a more time-consuming process. Furthermore, there is not enough trading and what there is seems to be mostly local. As a result, even when there is good news released about a company, there is not much of an effect on the stock price. There also appears to be no correlation between earnings and the price of stocks listed there.

The ASE provides a much-needed avenue for raising funds for start-up or emerging companies but these are not the types of companies in which you will be investing. Investment in these companies is best left to the venture capitalists, gamblers and dreamers. You will only deal in established, actively-traded stocks.

I have never traded on the Montreal Stock Exchange. This is more a result of living in Calgary rather than any indisposition towards the exchange. Consequently, I do not know enough about trading there to give any helpful comments. Besides, I find I have enough to do watching Toronto and Vancouver without adding to my daily workload.

2) One Security at a Time - At first you should only deal with one security at a time, that is, close out one transaction before entering into another. Just like an athlete you must start out slowly until top conditioning is attained. You probably will modify this rule fairly quickly, for as you gain more experience you will likely be trading in three to five (or more) securities at any given time.

3) No More Than 20% - Invest no more than 20% of your capital in any one issue. In fact, possibly consider only investing 10% if your pool of funds is large enough that 10% will allow you to purchase a board lot.

Although experienced speculators will invest as much as their instincts dictate, I usually try to stick to the 20% rule myself. It is seldom that I invest over 40%.

In Section III you will find a rule that dictates the maximum number of shares you can buy of a given stock. This rule may preclude you from investing any more than 20% of your capital in any event.

4) **Never Buy IPOs or New Issues** - You only want to be trading in active listed stocks. If you start buying initial public offerings (IPOs) or new issues, you have no idea if they are priced right to generate positive market interest. Once these stocks obtain a market listing there will be time enough for you to decide if you want to buy them.

5) Never Buy What a Broker is Selling - Whenever I break this rule it usually costs me money. But before the brokers get together and put out a hit on me, let me qualify it.

First, this rule applies only to this system, i.e. speculative stocks. Therefore I am saying never buy stocks of a speculative nature that a broker is pushing. This system is going to tell you what stocks you should be buying, so why buy anything else? Any quality, investment-grade issues he may be suggesting must certainly be taken under consideration for your other long term investment objectives.

Second, as previously mentioned, 40% of all brokers have less than four years' experience. As you become more adept at using this system you probably will have a better success ratio at picking winning speculative stocks than your broker will.

Third, your broker could be recommending a stock to you for any one of a multitude of reasons. His company may be underwriting the stock; he may have just been to a show-and-tell given by the promoters and he was impressed; his company may have a position in the stock and is trying to sell it off (or worse he may have a position); his company's analysts may have just come out with a good report on the company and he believes you may profit from this; he may have just seen a good news release in the stock dailies and figures it bodes well for the company. These are just a few examples of why he may be touting the stock but there could be a myriad of others. No matter what his reasons or how good his intentions are, if the stock does not fit all the parameters of this system, you should not be buying it.

I suggest you take the stock under advisement and monitor it daily. You will know when the buying public decides it's a good issue. If this never happens you have taken no risk. If it does happen your risk is reduced when you buy because the stock will already be beginning to move.

Fourth, if the issue your broker is selling is a new issue, you shouldn't be buying it anyway. Remember, you are only supposed to be buying listed, actively-traded stocks.

Finally, if he is selling a currently-listed and actively-traded stock, and you feel you just can't pass it up, be sure to follow the rules of "When to Sell" in Section III and when you decide it's time to sell, don't let anybody talk you out of it.

Again, this rule only applies to the speculative portion

of your portfolio and in this context I suggest you never break it.

6) Never Break the Rules - This is not as simple as it may sound. I don't think there are many of us who do not let our emotions get involved in our decision-making from time to time. Wait until you start selling out positions at a loss and see what emotions you experience.

I do not expect that you will be able to stick to the rules 100% of the time, however, the more you can exert discipline over yourself to follow the rules the more successful you will be. This is one instance where rules are NOT made to be broken.

GENERAL THOUGHTS

Many of you may ask, "If everyone follows this system, who is left to invest in new or emerging companies or stocks that do not meet the parameters?" The answer is, almost everybody.

Most people who read this book will probably decide it takes too much time and effort to put into practice. This does not mean they will not receive any benefit, for they will certainly gain some education and if they find out that they are not suited to stock market speculation, they can invest their money in other areas that are more suited to their temperament.

Successful speculation is an art not a science. It requires that one develop experience, judgement, instinct, diligence and discipline. It also takes time. Unfortunately there are many who cannot develop the necessary traits to speculate effectively. If this book can help you to discover whether or not you can be a speculator, I will consider it a success.

Of all the traits a speculator must have, I consider discipline to be of paramount importance. The inability to stick to the rules of the game at all costs will lead to your downfall more quickly than any other factor.

Now let's begin!

SUMMARY OF GENERAL RULES

- Only trade the TSE.

- Trade only one security at a time when you first begin.

- Invest no more than 20% of your capital in any one issue.

- Never buy IPOs or new issues.

- Only buy stocks selected by yourself.

- Never buy what a broker is selling.

- Never break the rules.

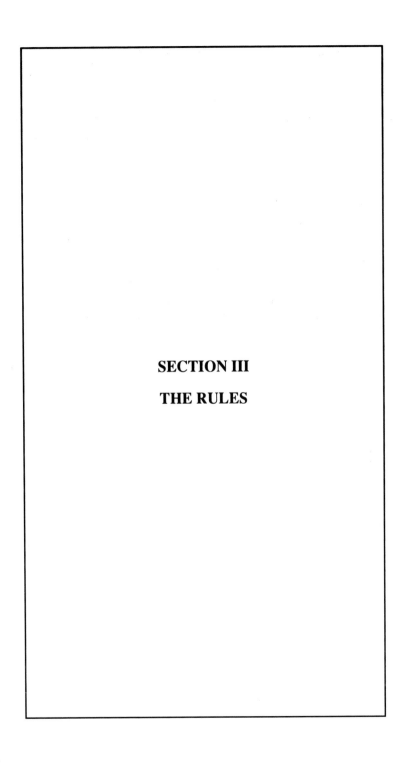

SECTION III

THE RULES

HOW TO BUY

On page 30, I listed the key elements of this system. It is now time to see what these elements mean and how to apply them.

MARKET ACTION, POSITION AND DEPTH

Market Action is determined by two essential components - price and volume movement. Market position is determined by where a stock's price lies relative to its 52-week Hi-Low. Market Depth (or Breadth) is gauged by how widely a particular stock is held or by how many transactions constitute the daily trading volume. As you read further, these elements will be defined more clearly.

If the trading volume of a stock is increasing and the price is increasing in conjunction with this increased volume, it is an indicator that the buying public has become bullish on this stock. It is impossible to predict how long this bullish attitude will be maintained but the parameters discussed in the "When to Sell" segment of this section will indicate when it is coming to an end.

Both *The Globe* and *The Financial Post* list the most active stocks and the stocks with the largest percentage price change in summary boxes in their daily stock listings for the TSE. *The Post* lists this information for the Montreal and Vancouver exchanges as well, while *The Globe* only lists the most active stocks on these exchanges. *The Globe* lists the top value leaders while *The Post* lists the top net gainers and losers.

As informative as these summaries are, you cannot do this

system justice by only pursuing the stocks listed there. Usually you will find that the largest percentage gains are made by lower priced stocks while the most active stocks are the higher priced issues. Although I quickly skim this section in case there should happen to be any quick picks that follow the rules, I then do my daily scan of the rest of the listings. If all the listings are not considered you will miss stocks that have a good combination of volume and price change, not just one or the other.

The following shows how to scan the daily stock pages and pick stocks with the best potential gain.

a) Scan the price change column and look for any stocks that have increased significantly over the prior day's trading. By "significantly" I mean the following:

Stock Price	% Change
$ 0.50 - $ 1.99	15 or greater
$ 2.00 - $ 9 7/8	10 "
$10.00 - $19 7/8	5 "
over $20.00	3 "

Circle any stocks that fall within these guidelines. These parameters may be modified as your judgement and instincts improve with experience but they should be followed closely when you are just beginning.

Applying percentages to stocks trading below $0.50 is irrelevant, for it is not uncommon to see these stocks make moves in excess of 50% - but who really cares that a ten cent stock has gone to fifteen? Even though it has increased 50%, it still does not indicate any particular bullishness about the stock. If it has gone from ten cents to thirty or forty cents, you may want to look at it, but you should still tread with extreme caution.

b) Check the volume on the stocks you have circled. Any which have traded less than 20,000 shares should be eliminated. Although I am setting 20,000 shares as the lower limit, I generally prefer the volume to exceed 50,000.

Another factor you should consider, relative to trading volume, is how thinly or broadly a stock is held. This information is readily available through your broker. When a stock is thinly-held, the bulk of the issued stock is in the hands of very few people, whereas broadly-held stocks have a large ownership base. If the stock is thin, small volumes or very few transactions can generate disproportionate moves in price but a stock that is widely-held will usually exhibit a closer relationship between price and volume movement.

Attention also should be given to how much stock can be considered free-trading. For example, 10,000,000 shares of a stock may be issued but 8,000,000 may be in the hands of three or four people. This leaves only 2,000,000 shares that can really be considered free-trading. Market action may be initiated by the holders of the 8,000,000 shares, but it will usually be the owners of the 2,000,000 shares that will prolong it. It is the activity of the trading in the free-trading shares that will indicate how bullish a market is in a particular stock. Obviously 100,000 shares traded in a stock with

2,000,000 free-trading shares will be more significant than the same volume traded in a stock with 10,000,000 free-trading shares. Information relative to the capitalization of a company, i.e. authorized and issued stock, can be obtained through your broker.

With experience you will look at the above two rules together. Sometimes the price change will fall marginally short of the percentage change guidelines but the volume suggests that a very bullish outlook is developing for a particular stock. If a stock's price has risen only 8% or 9% on extremely large volume do not reject it just because the rules say it must go up 10%. Remember, these are only guidelines. This a case where the rules must be bent. It is the combination of price and volume movement that is most important and they must be considered together. Conversely, if the volume is borderline but the price change is substantial, I would enter it into my worksheet as a stock to monitor and when the activity increases consider buying. If the bullish interest is real the stock will eventually meet your parameters. At no time should you consider buying stocks when the price increases substantially but the volume is small.

c) Find out how many transactions constituted the trading volume. Once again, this information is available through your broker. You do not want to buy a stock where the volume was established by very few trades. You want to be sure that there is a broad general interest in the stock - 100,000 shares traded by twenty people is much more preferable than if it were traded by three or four. In fact, if it were only traded by three or four, you should not buy it.

If you look in *The Globe* in the summ
"Toronto Market Statistics," you will fin
entitled "Market Breadth." This section sh
many issues were traded and how many tran.   ⸱ɔ
took place. By dividing the number of issues traded
into the total number of transactions, you can determine the average number of trades per issue. The
number of transactions for the stock or stocks in which
you are interested should equal or exceed this average.

It is possible that large trading volumes on low transaction numbers could be a precursor of good things to
come because knowledgeable buyers may be establishing positions early. Although I do not recommend
buying these stocks, I would definitely advise putting
them in your worksheet as stocks to monitor.

d) Check the 52-week High-Low range for the stocks you
have remaining:

i) Eliminate all stocks making new highs. By buying
stocks making new highs you incur the risk that these
stocks may have peaked and will soon begin to
decline. It is next to impossible to predict how much
higher these stocks will go if, in fact, they will
continue to rise at all. Although there are many
astute speculators who make a good living playing
nothing but stocks making new highs, the prime
objective here is to decrease risk as much as possible. You will not, therefore, buy these stocks when
you first start following this system.

After you have been trading for a year or two, you

may wish to begin trading these types of stocks and feel you can accept the higher risks involved. When you do, you must take into consideration the "When to Sell" parameters. If the stock is not exhibiting any of the sell signs discussed there, you can be reasonably sure a top has not been reached, although you will still have no idea of how much higher the stock will go. If the continuing rise is short-lived the risk versus gain may not have been worth the effort - it could also turn out to be another Stikine Resources or Hemlo Gold Mines.

ii) Eliminate all stocks that have risen higher than one half the difference between the high and the low. For example, if the high is $10 and the low is $5 the stock cannot be priced over $7 1/2.

At this point I am going to make an arbitrary statement:

> When a stock begins a solid bull run, it is anticipated that it will eventually make new highs.

Using this guideline it is assumed that the stock will at least rise to its previous 52-week high. Since you only want to buy stocks with the potential to make minimum gains of 50% - 100%, the difference between the price you pay and the 52-week high must at least allow you to potentially earn a percentage in this range. Therefore, if a stock has a $5 low and a $10 high, the maximum you should be paying is about $6 1/2. At this price, if the stock goes to $10 you would make just over 50% profit. This maximum that you are willing to pay should be entered into your worksheet. When it has been surpassed you should stop buying, even if you have not acquired all the stock you wanted (see comments on pyramiding in Section II under "Buying").

Another rule of thumb that you should consider is this:

> Consistent strength and volume after a long period of general decline will usually indicate a bull run is about to begin.

Therefore, it would be preferable if you could find stocks that have been trading at or near their 52-week low for an extended period and are now starting to move off it. You should ask your broker to check the trading history of stocks in which you are interested and find out when the lows were actually established. The fact that a stock does not exhibit this particular characteristic should not preclude you from buying it. If it does, however, your confidence level should be increased and you may want to take a larger position than normal.

After you have taken all of the above factors into consideration, you should enter the stocks remaining on your list into your rough work sheet, as shown in the Appendix. You will record the date, name of the stock, 52-week high-low, high-low for that date, closing price and the number of shares traded. Normally you will find that only about three to five stocks will fit these parameters. Some days you will find none.

It is now time to call your broker to place the order. You should first check the market about fifteen minutes after the open. If the stock(s) you are interested in are looking aggressive then place your order. If not, you should wait for an hour or two after the market is opened to see if trading in the stock(s) is going to continue to follow the previous day's bullish pattern. If the stock is trading below the previous day's level, don't buy it. If the price is about the same as the previous day continue to monitor the stock until it exhibits further bullish strength, which will justify buying it, or begins to decline, thus allowing you to eliminate it from your list. Make notes on your rough work sheet that indicate why you did not buy a particular stock, reasons for continuing to monitor it, or any other information you may have learned from your investigation.

If the price of the stock is up and there is active trading, take the plunge - but how deep?

First, buy no more than 10% and preferably no more than 5% of the previous day's trading volume. This will hopefully ensure that when you decide to sell, the number of shares you own can easily be absorbed in one day's trading. This is a rule I try never to break and I suggest you don't either. It can be a very frustrating experience being unable to liquidate a position because the market cannot absorb the number of shares you hold.

Secondly, only invest up to 20% of your speculative pool of funds. This precaution is taken to preserve your capital for buying other issues. Until you have gained enough experience and confidence in your ability to trade speculatively, you should not risk more capital than this. Once you have determined that you have the disposition and temperament to take higher risks, you can set this limit at any level you feel comfortable with, although, as I mentioned previously, I think 40% should be your absolute maximum. Remember, however, no matter how much capital you are prepared to risk, never buy more than 10% of the previous day's trading volume.

You now know what stock you want to buy, the maximum you will pay for it, and how many shares you want. The only question remaining is - how do you go about establishing your desired position?

You first look at the bid and offer and see where they lie relative to what you are willing to pay. If they are substantially lower than your set maximum find out from your broker how much stock is available on the offer. If there is enough stock to fill the position you want, simply buy at that level. When enough stock is not available, you buy what is there. You can get the rest of the stock you want in one of four ways. The way you choose will be directed by how strongly the stock meets the buy parameters and, therefore, how bullish your attitude is towards the stock. You can join the current bid, raise the current bid, bid at the offer at which you bought the first portion of your position, or meet the next offered price, which can have the additional benefit of creating more bullish action.

When the bid and offer are close to your maximum, you do not have much room to pursue the stock. In this case, I would again find out how much stock is offered and if there is enough to fill my requirements, simply buy. If there is not enough stock available, I would take out what is offered and either join the current bid or raise it slightly in order to obtain the balance. If the next offer coming out is still below my maximum, I would then increase my bid to that level and complete my acquisition. In this case, you discuss it with your broker and tell him you will buy up to a certain price (your maximum) until your order is filled. If you are unable to get all the stock you initially wanted it makes no matter. The stock may perform extremely well and you can possibly look at pyramiding later on (see "Pyramiding" in Section II).

I know everybody wants to buy stock as cheaply as possible and will always tend to bid lower than the current offer. To me, there is conflicting logic here. First, why be worried about nickels and dimes when you believe the stock is going on a bull run? Second, why put any downward pressure on a stock that you want to continue its bull run? Remember, the best stocks are hard to buy but easy to sell (see Section II), therefore if sellers are dropping down to the bid, perhaps the stock is too easy to buy.

You should now enter your purchases into a ledger sheet like the one in the Appendix named "Transactions." This will be your record of all the trades you have made and the profits or losses on these trades.

You should also set up a third ledger that keeps track of the overall position of your speculative account. An example of this is shown in the Appendix as well. It is a brief summary of your "Transaction" record and monitors the cash position of your account at any given time.

OTHER CONSIDERATIONS

There are other factors that I consider to be of lesser importance and I usually do not let them have a major effect on my decisions to buy. They can, however, increase your comfort level.

The first of these is the Price Earnings Ratio (P/E). In my early years of investing in the stock market, I used to use a P/E of 10 as my rule of thumb. This meant that if a company had earned $1.00 per share, the price of its stock would be $10.00. I felt that any stock trading below a P/E of 10 would be considered a bargain and any stock trading over 10 was possibly over-priced. That was in 1966. Today it is not quite that simple.

Each industry has a P/E range that is particular to itself and what is acceptable at any given time is subject to change. For example, a P/E of around 20 is generally acceptable for a totally integrated oil company today, yet in the early 1980s, when the National Energy Policy created a crunch for the industry, P/Es of the order of 10 or 11 were prevalent.

Mining stocks, in particular gold stocks, may have P/Es in the 40 - 60 range. This is because more weight is given to a mining company's ability to make a return on invested capital through the development of its reserves or its ability to increase its reserves, than is given to its actual earnings per share. Because of the large amounts of capital required to find and develop economic ore bodies, much of the revenue generated from a mine, especially during the early years of production, is considered to be a return of this capital rather than a component of net income. As a result, reported earnings per share can be relatively low compared to the actual cash flow generated. You therefore see mining companies showing losses yet still trading in the $10 to $15

67

range. Comparing a mining company's cash flow to its price per share will give you a more realistic picture of its true value. You should also look at its net asset value per share. If a company is depleting its reserves without replacing them through new exploration, you will find the price begin to decrease. (Integrated oil company stocks usually are priced according to a combination of reserves and earnings from operations.)

Acceptable P/Es for industrials may be in the 10 - 20 range, yet forest and paper products may fall in the 5 - 10 range. Once again these ranges are always subject to change. I am only trying to give you examples of how P/Es can vary for different industries, not establish guidelines for you to follow. The P/E average for any particular group of companies in the TSE 300 Index can be obtained from your broker.

Previously, I said that in the early days of my investing I felt that a P/E of less than 10 possibly indicated a bargain and over 10 possibly indicated a stock was overpriced. In reality this is not the case.

P/Es are calculated using the current price but last year's earnings. Thus, if it is anticipated that a company's earnings will be better than the previous year, the price of the stock will increase and consequently so will the P/E. Therefore a higher than average P/E could be a good sign and a low P/E (if it is anticipated earnings will drop) a bad sign. Accordingly, earnings forecasts must be taken into consideration when using P/Es as a parameter for investing in a stock. A low P/E could mean that a stock has been overlooked by the market if it appears the company's earnings are going to increase.

Other factors, such as a company's debt to equity ratio, general economic condition of a particular industry, etc., may all have an affect on a company's P/E. I treat it fairly lightly when I am buying a stock. It is the stock's actual performance that is most important.

It is also of interest to check the previous one or two week's Hi-Low, close and trading volume. I usually keep the weekly trading summaries on hand from *The Globe* or *The Post* for the previous three weeks, so that I can quickly check recent past trading.

Although I have previously said that things of lesser importance are being considered here, there are circumstances that can make checking recent trading very important. A good example is the situation where a stock has been making new lows over the past week or two. I would be very cautious about buying a stock merely on the fact that it has had one good day; for just as stock prices do not rise continually during a bull run they do not usually fall straight down when the bear walks through the door. They can have brief periods of support at various levels on the way down the same as a stock on the way up can have various levels of resistance.

If, on the other hand, the stock has been showing gradual increases in trading volume and the price has stabilized or is showing minor increases, it is very possible that it has been gathering steam for a major upward push. In this case, if the stock is well positioned relative to its 52-week Hi-Low and all other parameters look strong, I would be investing with quite a high degree of confidence.

You should let recent weeks' trading seriously affect your

decision to buy only if there is something extraordinary about it, as in the instances just mentioned. If a stock has been casually chugging along with nothing exciting happening and then one day falls within your buying parameters, perhaps the excitement is about to begin.

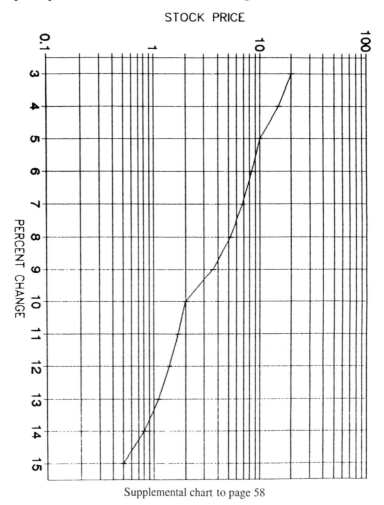

Supplemental chart to page 58

WHEN TO SELL

Buying stocks is only half the game. In order to win you must also sell. It is the profit gained from your sells that indicates how well you have played the game.

Making a decision on whether to sell or hold a stock probably wreaks more havoc, psychologically, on a player than any other play in the game, especially if he is faced with taking a loss. Many people have a tendency to look at paper profits as real profits but never look at paper losses as real losses. They mistakenly believe that until they sell, they have not really lost any money. They continue to live with the hope that the stock will recover and no real monetary loss will be incurred. This way of thinking will ALWAYS get you into trouble eventually.

How often have you seen friends or associates celebrating a major gain in a stock although they have not actually taken the profit by selling? You then discover, weeks or months later, that they still hold the stock and it is trading at a level much lower than when they were celebrating, or worse, at a level lower than that at which they bought in the first place. Their problem was that they did not have any guidelines that would tell them when to sell. Unfortunately, the paper-loss belief discussed above may now have been triggered and they will not sell, thereby possibly adding to their woes. They may now feel locked into the stock. However, being locked into a stock is only a state of mind that you must learn to overcome.

This brings me to the most important rule you must learn to follow:

ACCEPT YOUR LOSSES AND ACCEPT THEM QUICKLY!

This rule probably will be the most difficult to obey because of the psychological barriers most of us have against taking losses, yet it is crucial to the preservation of your capital. There are many people who will read this manual who, by their nature, will be unable to accept losses. You will find out very quickly if you are one of these people after you have begun trading. If you cannot change this attitude, **GET OUT OF THE MARKET!**

It is a fallacy to think that what goes down is going to come back up. It is better to take the money you have remaining after taking a loss and put it back to work earning money instead of continuing to sit on an idle stock that may never recover.

I will now lay down the guidelines you should follow when deciding whether or not to sell a particular stock.

THE 10% - 20% LOSS RULE

When purchasing a stock you should establish at the outset how much you are prepared to lose. This may sound like a negative approach to buying a stock you think is going to appreciate but remember, you are probably going to be wrong more often than you will be right. By establishing the maximum amount you are prepared to lose when you first enter into a transaction, you preserve the remainder of your capital for future purchases. This is the crux of the "Accept your losses" rule.

I recommend that you set your loss at no more than 10% of your investment for higher-priced stocks and 20% for lower-priced stocks. Higher-priced stocks, for the purposes of starting this system, will be those whose price is greater than $5.00. I would also suggest that initially you keep your losses in the 10% - 15% range on all stocks. After you become more proficient at using this system you may set your guidelines at levels that you feel are more comfortable. AT NO TIME SHOULD YOUR LOSS BE SET HIGHER THAN 20% IN ANY ISSUE.

Once you have established a loss limit, STICK TO IT, no matter how you may be tempted to do otherwise from time to time. If your timing is wrong and the stock starts to rise at a later date you can always get back into it then, even if it means having to pay more than you sold it for. As you can see, a great amount of discipline and character will have to be exercised here.

You now know what to do when a stock does not live up to your expectations: SELL AND CUT YOUR LOSSES! But what do you do when a stock does perform according to plan? When, why and how do you sell?

A simple rule of thumb is to use the 10% - 20% loss rule. Anytime the stock exhibits downward movement of this magnitude simply sell. Although there is safety in this play you probably will not maximize your profits because when a stock starts a bull run it does not just rise continually. Its general trend is up but it usually accomplishes this through a series of increases and decreases. Over all, however, the increases are consistently greater than the decreases. If you were to chart the performance of a stock on a bull run it would exhibit a sawtooth picture like the one shown on the following page.

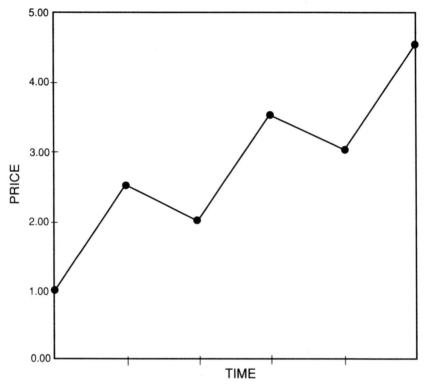

Therefore, a much more sophisticated strategy must be developed that will allow you to continue to ride your gains yet minimize the risk of losing your profits. The following is a summary of various conditions that can occur that will tell you when it is time to sell, or danger is not far down the road. Until one of these conditions arises you should continue to hold and ride with the market.

SELL INDICATORS

a) Volume is increasing - price is falling:

This is the grand-daddy of sell indicators, i.e. the

biggest danger signal of them all. A general sell-off is occurring and real trouble, if it is not already present, is not far ahead. BAIL OUT!!! Uninformed buying is still occurring but it is probably about to dry up. The traders who are in the know could be aware of impending bad news that the general public does not know about yet; the stock may have reached levels that are unable to be sustained because of purely technical or fundamental factors; the bull run may merely have just lost steam as a result of over-buying; there may be a sell-off due to profit-taking. Whatever the reason, the bloom is off the rose and it is time to get out.

b) Price is rising - Volume is decreasing or levelling off: When this occurs you should start to sell off your position unless condition (ii) below is present. Depending upon how much stock you own, possibly sell 25% - 50% initially. If the situation persists, gradually divest yourself of the rest of your stock.

i) This condition may indicate buying is drying up and the price is probably going to start falling soon. The price is likely being maintained because smaller, uninformed buyers are still acquiring positions in the stock. Once their orders are filled the price will probably weaken.

ii) It is also possible that the volume is shrinking because current position holders are settling in and waiting for greater gains. This creates a situation where there is still a large number of buy orders but few sell orders. Your broker may be able to determine if this is, in fact, the case. If so, continue to hold until other indicators arise that tell you it is time to sell.

c) Price is decreasing - Volume is decreasing:

This condition naturally follows condition (b) if the reason for (b) was situation (i). If you haven't already divested yourself of your position, DO IT NOW! This situation is almost as bad as sell indicator (a). In fact, it probably indicates conditions are soon to change into situation (a).

People who bought into the stock at the higher levels have not yet begun to panic and therefore are not selling in anticipation that this is just a temporary lull in the bull run and prices will soon start to rise again. It is just a matter of time, if the price continues to decrease, before panic will set in and a general sell-off will be launched.

d) Rate of price increase slows down or price stabilizes - Volume is still large:
Whenever a stock is on a bull run, plateaus occur at various levels where buyers are reluctant to continue buying at higher prices. These plateaus are called resistance levels. Public psychology seems to arbitrarily create these resistance levels, even though a stock may fundamentally appear to be worth more. Once a particular level is broken the price usually will rise again until a new resistance level is reached. This phenomenon is very evident with stocks that are reaching new highs. The fear that the stock is becoming overpriced starts to play a prominent role in determining price levels.

The real difficulty in ascertaining what action to take under these conditions lies in assessing whether it is a top or a resistance level that has been reached. If a top has been hit, you obviously want to liquidate your position, but if it is a resistance level, you want to continue to ride with the gains that are likely to ensue when the resistance is overcome.

My first suggestion is that if you are in doubt and have already made substantial profits in the stock, sell all or at least some of your position. If your instincts (which will improve with experience) tell you that it is a resistance level and not a top, monitor the stock for awhile. If the situation persists for more than a week or so, sell out. If the public is accumulating stock while the price marks time, trouble is probably not far ahead. Even if you decide to stay with the stock for awhile, you may want to sell off some of your holdings in any event, so that part of your profits are preserved if, in fact, a top has been reached. If it turns out that it was only a resistance level, you will still have a position to keep riding gains.

It is also possible that while you are monitoring the stock one of the other conditions discussed in this section will arise and you will know exactly what action should be taken.

e) **Volume is decreasing - Price is stabilizing or rate of increase is slowing down:** This condition probably indicates a top is soon to be reached. Buying is likely drying up and the bull run is over. I would liquidate my position at this time. The possibility still exists that the market is taking a brief pause before continuing its bull run but I think the odds are against it. Buy and sell orders are possibly weighted a little more heavily on the sell side. Even if it turns out that buys still outweigh sells, there will usually not be large enough further price advances to merit taking the risk that a top has been, or is about to be, reached and the market will begin to decline.

f) Gap between bid and offer is increasing:
When this occurs, you can be sure buying interest has really died. Trading volume will usually have tapered off substantially by this time. There are still some buyers who feel that buying at the bid price will still leave some room for profit but the public in general obviously thinks no profit can be made if stock is bought at the offered price.

Most of the time, the people who are offering the stock do not want to take a loss and have a strong reluctance to meet the bid price. Once these sellers resign themselves to the fact that they will not be able to sell at the price they want, they will start selling at the bid, thereby causing the price to tumble even further. In other words, it has become a buyers' market. The stock will eventually drop to a stabilized level and trading will become either sporadic or non-existent.

I have found that most of the time there is very little volume asked for on the bid side when this condition is prevalent so it is very difficult, if not impossible, to dispose of large positions. If you have been following all the other sell indicators or warning signs discussed in this section, you should never end up holding a stock that has reached this state. (As an aside, you should obviously never buy a stock that has a large gap between bid and offer.)

You should be made aware that often the bid is what I consider artificial. In penny stocks, the promoters or major share holders (usually one and the same) do not like to see their stock listed without a bid. They, therefore, will make a bid for a board lot so that it would appear that some buying interest still exists. This bid will usually be low enough that they do not mind if it is filled.

It should be remembered that the stocks you have been buying were bought because it appeared that fairly quick gains could be realized. These stocks (if you have chosen properly) made rapid gains and could fall just as rapidly. You must therefore monitor them closely and frequently (read daily) and be prepared to sell quickly if any of the sell indicators or warning signals arise.

When you decide to sell your position you want, of course, to get the best possible price. I suggest you sell in one of two ways. Either offer your stock at just below the currently offered price or meet the bid price. If you choose to meet the bid price, check on how much stock is wanted at that price. If the amount is large enough to take out your position, great. If not, you may want to offer at various levels between the bid and ask until all your stock is sold.

Unless you are really anxious or desperate to sell, never make a market sell. You have no control over the disposition of your stock and you possibly may get some unpleasant surprises.

Several years ago, a friend of mine wanted to liquidate his position in a poorly performing stock. He had bought most of it in the $0.90 to $1.20 range and the stock was being offered at $0.80 and bid at $0.70. He placed a market sell for 10,000 shares. When the dust had cleared, some of his stock had sold as low as $0.50. When it had all been taken out, the bid-ask was back to $0.70 - $0.78. I can only say, "Beware of the Wolves!"

MONEY MANAGEMENT

Throughout this book, various rules have been established that determine how much stock you should buy, how much money you should invest, and the maximum loss you will accept in any one transaction. Although most of these topics were discussed in the context of market considerations, they all have a direct relationship to good money management. The way in which you manage your money relative to the risk undertaken will determine your financial success. There-fore, at the risk of appearing repetitious, I will establish some investment guidelines, which I feel will help you achieve that success.

The first order of business is to designate a portion of your total investment portfolio to speculative ventures. Although I feel you can be quite effective dedicating an amount between $5000 - $20,000, some of you may want to risk more or less. Conservative investors should probably only risk up to 20% of their total investment capital but there are those who have the temperament, attitude, aptitude and experience to risk much more. Whatever amount you choose to start with, it should not be so large as to affect your lifestyle should you lose it all.

After you have decided how much you want to speculate with, open a separate trading account with these funds. This will enable you to keep your speculative funds segregated from your normal investment funds. This is important because once this fund is established, with two exceptions, you are not to add more to it. The two exceptions are as follows:

1) After you have begun trading, if you find you are capable of taking greater risks you may increase the fund. You will only do this once!

2) Each year your total pool of investment funds will likely increase (usually as a result of higher income or savings). If, for example, you initially started with 20% of your investment funds dedicated to speculation, you may wish to add 20% of your extra funds to the pool. Only do this once per year.

You will likely find that there will be no necessity to add to your initial fund unless you decide to become more aggressive. Only time and experience can determine this.

Until you become proficient and are prepared to take larger risks, you should not invest more than 20% of your initial fund in any one issue. If you are a beginner, you should trade for at least one year before increasing this percentage. By that time, you should have developed a reasonable assessment of your risk-taking capabilities.

As your fund grows, you can establish different benchmarks for investment limits from time to time. I would suggest reevaluating every six months. For example, if you started with $20,000, your maximum investment in any one issue would be $4000. If your fund grows to $30,000, you can then set your limit at $6,000. Once a limit has been established, you should try not to invest less than this amount, although circumstances may arise that preclude you from doing so.

You may ask, "If my investment fund is shrinking, why don't I decrease my investment limit?" The answer is:

because you will pick more losers than winners and you need to give every investment an equal opportunity to make money. The following example will illustrate this.

Suppose you make five choices in five weeks and the first four choices are wrong and the fifth is right. (Remember, you are buying stocks you feel have the potential to double and the 10% - 20% loss rule will be implemented on the losers.) Because you are only just starting, you will set your loss limit at 10% and assume the winner only goes up 50%.

Week	Invested	Gain/(loss)	Balance
1	$4000	($400)	$19,600
2	$4000	($400)	$19,200
3	$4000	($400)	$18,800
4	$4000	($400)	$18,400
5	$4000	$2000	$20,400

As you can see, even though you were right only once you have made $400. This is a 2% profit in five weeks, which equates to a 20.8% return annually. If you had been investing on a decreasing balance, your last investment would have been $3680 and your gain would have been $1840 for a profit of only $240. The above example is overly simplified because it does not take brokerage fees into account. In fact, you would have accumulated a small loss if this had been done.

The previous example showed what could happen if you only had a 20% success rate. But watch how quickly your profits accumulate as the success rate grows. (Assume your fund is $20,000 and you make one trade per week).

Weeks	Success Rate	Profit	Annualized
40	20%	$3,200	20.8%
40	25%	$8,000	52.0%
40	30%	$12,800	83.2%
40	35%	$17,600	114.4%
40	40%	$22,400	145.6%

I have used forty weeks as a trading period so as to obtain an exact number of trades. The key issue here is that by cutting losses and riding gains, good rates of return can be made even though you are wrong more often than not.

Well, so much for the ideal world. In the real world you do not lose 10% - 20% every time you are wrong nor do you make 50% or more when you are right. As you will see in the trading example in the Appendix, when you select a stock wrongly, although it is possible it will decline 10% - 20% right off, it usually trades up or down marginally. In other words, it just does not perform at all. Since the stock is not performing you will most likely be selling it at levels where you either just lose the brokerage commission plus a small capital loss or make enough to just cover commissions plus a small gain. When a stock does perform well you will normally make a profit of 10% - 20% with the odd trade earning 100% or more. Regardless of how the real world behaves, you should still make returns on investment of the order shown in the example.

I would expect that you should be trading with a success rate of 25% - 30% within one year. By this I mean you will be selecting with this frequency stocks that do better than break even and will enable you to earn returns similar to those shown in the idealized table for this success rate. So you can see it is not necessary to invest more than 20% of your total funds to be successful and, in addition, when your picks are wrong your fund decreases only marginally.

I expect (unless you are exceptionally lucky) that you will select wrongly quite often initially but don't get discouraged. Persistence and discipline will eventually pay-off.

Whatever amount you set as your investment limit, stick to it. If you do not, your losses will not be proportionate to your gains. It is obvious that if you invest 100% of your funds one time and incur a 10% loss, your loss is five times as large as if you had only invested 20%. In order to make a proper rate of return you would have to continue investing at the 100% level, which also would mean injecting further capital to maintain your fund.

As your fund grows, there will be times when you cannot invest your limit. Earlier in the book a rule was stated that allowed you to buy only 5% - 10% of the previous day's volume. Suppose your fund has grown to $30,000 and your investment limit is $6000. A stock has traded 50,000 shares at $1.00. The most you could buy would be 5000 shares, i.e. $5000 worth.

Often there will be no stocks that fall within the parameters for buying. Do not get impatient. Unless the opportunity exists to buy an issue that has the potential for large gains, it is better to let your cash sit and earn interest. There is no point in buying idle stocks just to keep invested.

Eventually you must make a decision as to how large your fund can be and still be effective. It will become harder and harder to keep it fully invested - especially in a bear market. In a bull market you can easily keep two or three hundred thousand dollars invested but you may be hard-pressed to keep even one hundred thousand working in a bear market. Any time you find this situation occurring you should place your excess funds in short term securities such as T-Bills or term deposits until market activity increases to the point that more product becomes available that fits your parameters.

There is a limit to how much money you can expect to double as a result of the market itself being unable to supply you with enough product. This limit will depend on how bearish or bullish the market is at any given time. No matter what the market is doing you can reasonably expect to double amounts up to 30 or 40 thousand dollars. If you have more than this you can still make returns of 30 - 40% but it will take your time and a lot of work. It is the striving to double your funds that will result in high returns. Shoot for the moon, you may at least land in a tree.

The main reason we invest money is to accumulate or preserve wealth. To accomplish this you should keep reinvesting your profits. But all work and no play makes Jack a dull boy. Therefore I say once a year reward yourself. Take 10% or 15% of your profits and treat yourself to a vacation or purchase some luxury item you have always wanted. It is no fun making money if you can't spend some of it.

BUYING SUMMARY

STOCK SELECTION

- Scan price change column and single out any stocks that have increased significantly over the prior day's trading.

- Check trading volumes on these stocks
  - Eliminate all which have traded less than 20,000 shares.
- Determine how many transactions constituted the trading volume.
  - Eliminate all where the number of transactions is less than twenty.

- Check the 52 Week High-Low range.
  - Eliminate all stocks making new highs.
  - Eliminate all stocks that have a price higher than one half the difference between the high and low.
  - Eliminate all stocks where the difference between the price of the stock and the high is less than 50% of the price of the stock.

HOW TO BUY

- Buy your selected stock(s) only if the market continues to be bullish. Do not buy if the stock opens the next day either down or with no change. Continue to check the action throughout the day.

- Only invest up to 20% of your total funds.

- Buy no more than 5% - 10% of the previous day's trading volume.

- Set a maximum price at which you will buy. Once this price is exceeded do not buy any more, even if you have not filled your desired position.

SELLING SUMMARY

- Cut your losses at 10% - 20% when you have made a wrong selection.

- Keep holding your stock as long as the price keeps rising and the volume is large.

- Avoid market sell orders.

SELL INDICATORS

- Volume is increasing - Price is falling.

- Price is rising - Volume is decreasing or levelling off.

- Price is decreasing - Volume is decreasing.

- Rate of price increase slows down or price stabilizes - Volume is still large.

- Volume is decreasing - Price is stabilizing or rate of increase is slowing down.

- Gap between bid and offer is increasing.

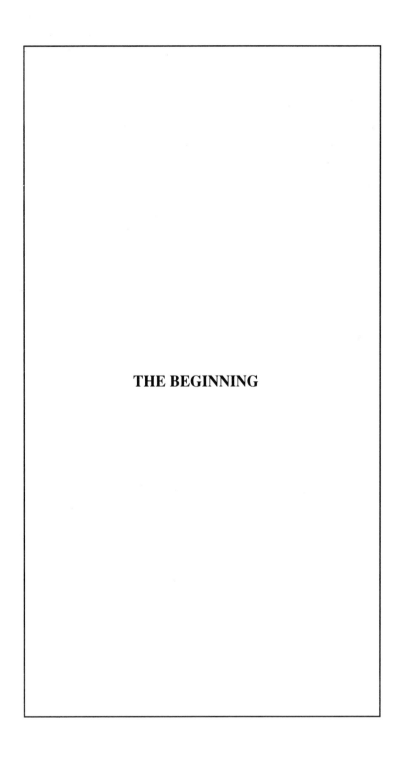

THE BEGINNING

THE BEGINNING

Well, there you have it. I have tried to present and discuss the fundamental components I think are essential to successful stock market speculation. If I have missed something, I hope it is minor and will not have any overall adverse effect on your ability to speculate like a winner.

I know there are many topics I have not covered, but they are more appropriate to a book on the stock market in general rather than a book of this nature, the purpose of which is to outline specific rules and guidelines for investing in the market in a speculative manner. Although one should have a good general knowledge of how the market works and some topics not discussed here certainly have value for general interest's sake, these things are not essential to the successful implementation of this system.

I have included an Appendix which shows an actual period of trading using this system. Stocks which were bought and sold during this period are not necessarily performing now, so I do not intend that you follow them. This Appendix is included only so that you may see the system at work and also derive some idea of the types of records you will need to keep so that you can analyze and track your stocks.

I am firm in my belief that if you spend the time required to follow this system and develop discipline, success will be yours. It's up to you now. You're on your own.

GOOD LUCK!

Ted Carter

September, 1991.

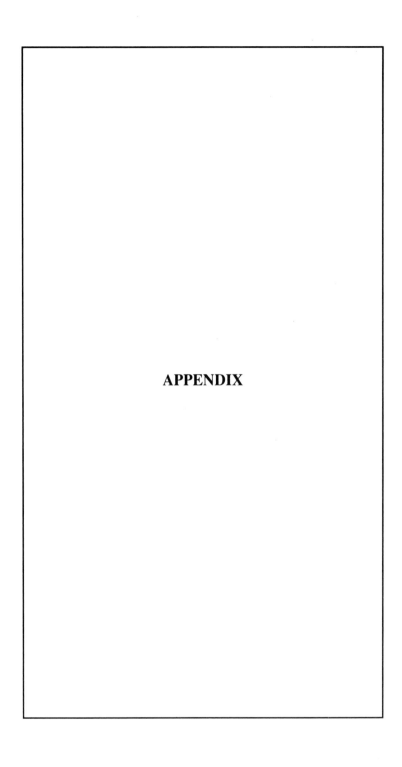

APPENDIX

APPENDIX NOTES

The trading period shown here was selected at random. As it turned out, it began in a bear market which bottomed the week of November 14. Even though trading began in a bear market, $2909.89 was earned for the period September 8 to November 9. This represents an annualized rate of return on investment of 87%. For the full five-month trading period to January 31, $14,378.71 was earned. This equates to an annualized rate of return of approximately 172%. It should also be noted that for the period January 17 to January 30,losses of well over $2000.00 were incurred which indicate that it is much harder to select stocks after the market has been bullish for awhile. This is because it is difficult to determine whether interest in a stock has actually become bullish or the stock is just a late trailer in a prolonged bull market. Therefore I suggest that you be very cautious in your approach to the market when it begins to appear that the bull may have run its course.

B - Buy   M - Monitor   X - No Further Interest

Prepared By / Prepare par	Initials / Initiales	Date
Approved By / Approuve par		

Date		Stock	DAY Hi	DAY Low	DAY Close	DAY Chge	DAY Volume	52-Week Hi	52-Week Low	Previous Week Hi	Previous Week Low	Previous Week Close	Previous Week Chge	Previous Week Volume	
1988															
Sep.6	~~M~~ X	Ekaton A	1.04	0.87	1.04	+14	161600	1.85	0.87	1.15	0.90	0.90	-12	186033	Sep.7 - Vol. good, No price - M Sep.8 - No. Vol. - No price X
	~~M~~ X	Moneta Porcupine	0.60	0.46	0.60	+15	49820	2.90	0.40	0.49	0.40	0.45	+1	160800	" " " - M " " " X
	~~M~~ X	Seagram	66 3/4	66 1/8	66 5/8	+5/8	58517	101 3/4	62	66 1/4	64 3/4	66	+7/8	290688	Sep.7 - Price change slow. Sep.9 - Vol. shrinking X
	X	Walwyn	5 5/8	4.80	5 3/8	+7/8	57112	9 3/4	3.85	4.70	4.50	4.70	+20	9154	Sep.7 - No action X
Sep.7	X	Nahanni	0.48	0.35	0.41	+11	27000	1.15	0.25	0.25	0.25	0.25	—	200	Sep.8 - 35 B - 40 A - no trades X
Sep.8	X	FPI Ltd.	10 1/2	9 7/8	10 3/8	+5/8	49450	19 3/4	9 1/4	9 7/8	9 1/2	9 7/8	+1/8	98696	Sep.9 - No vol. - price even X
	B	Golden Knight wt	2.20	1.80	2.15	+36	69900	3.70	0.80	1.80	1.60	1.80	+15	51800	Sep.9 - Bought 2000 @ 2.30
	X	Interquest	0.38	0.30	0.38	+13	40550	1.00	0.14	0.20	0.14	0.20	+5	38500	Sep.9 - Opened Down X
	B	SHL Systemhouse	8 5/8	7 7/8	8 1/2	+3/4	44600	32	7	7 1/2	7	7 1/8	-3/8	50241	Sep.9 - Bought 500 @ 9.00
Sep.9	X	Counsel wt	0.40	0.20	0.31	+20	46700	3.90	0.04	N/A	N/A	N/A	N/A	N/A	Unable to buy - Too much fluctuation
	~~M~~ X	Integra Systems	1.49	1.20	1.49	+34	19200	2.50	1.05	1.20	1.15	1.15	—	4000	Sep.12 - Opened Down X
Sep.12	~~M~~ X	Pacific Transocean	1.75	1.50	1.51	+36	281950	6 1/4	1.01	2.65	1.01	1.15	-1.65	10581	Making new lows - M
Sep.15	X	Counsel wt	0.55	0.40	0.55	+15	26900	3.90	0.04	0.40	0.04	0.31	+21	70450	Opened Down X
Sep.20	X	Golden Knight wt	1.75	1.45	1.60	+22	38450	3.65	0.80	2.10	1.61	1.65	-50	110000	Opened Down X
Sep.21	B M	Granges	3.70	3.45	3.70	+35	60600	15 7/8	3.35	4.15	3.35	3.90	-25	2630000	Hitting new lows - M Sep.22 Bought 1000 @ 3.85
Sep.22	X	Int'l Platinum	1.12	0.99	1.12	+15	26610	4.90	0.90	1.05	0.90	1.00	+5	51000	Opened Down X
Sep.26	~~M~~ X	Northair Mines	1.00	0.86	0.90	+13	104258	2.75	0.71	0.80	0.71	0.77	-3	76000	Opened Steady - M Weakened Sep.28 X
Sep.27	B	Ego Resources	0.50	0.45	0.50	+9	26000	2.73	0.35	0.45	0.37	0.37	-3	21000	Bought 7000 @ 0.57 - Sep.28
	X	Newhawk Gold	3.90	3.60	3.90	+40	24280	8 1/4	3.05	3.70	3.05	3.35	-25	205000	Opened Down X
Sep.28	X	Pacific Transocean	1.30	1.09	1.30	+18	58100	6	1.01	1.45	1.11	1.15	-18	303000	Opened Down X
Sep.29	X	Breakwater Res.	4.20	3.95	4.20	+30	70630	8 3/4	3.70	4.05	3.85	3.90	-15	129000	" " X
	B	Polysteel	1.05	0.90	1.05	+20	27200	6 1/4	0.80	1.00	0.80	0.90	-9	44000	Sep.30 - Bought 3500 @ 1.10
Sep.30	X	Jonpol	2.00	1.80	2.00	+30	26932	3.75	1.30	2.00	1.65	1.75	-25	90000	Opened Down - Low Volume X
Oct.3	B	Falconbridge	21 3/8	21	21 1/4	+7/8	266610	30 3/4	16 5/8	20 7/8	20 1/8	20 3/8	+1/8	483000	Oct.4 - Bought 200 @ 21 1/2
Oct.4	B	Golden Rule	1.85	1.56	1.85	+25	86900	8 5/8	1.55	1.80	1.55	1.58	-12	98000	Making new lows - M Oct.5 - Bought 2000 @ 2.00
	~~M~~ X	Scintilore	3.30	2.80	3.30	+40	31050	8 3/4	2.00	3.65	2.70	3.15	-40	139000	Questionable - M Oct.5 - Price stable - vol. good Oct.6 - Off X
Oct.5	X	Beverly Dev.	0.55	0.40	0.55	+17	43100	1.25	0.10	0.38	0.28	0.35	-3	73000	Oct.6 - Vol. off - No movement X
	~~M~~ X	Domtar	13 1/4	12 3/4	13 1/4	+5/8	30215	21 7/8	11 5/8	12 7/8	12 1/4	12 7/8	-5/8	43000	Oct.6 - Price steady Vol. steady Oct.7. +1 1/2 Can't Buy. Fully invested. Asked @ 15.

Prepared By / Préparé par	Initials / Initiales	Date
Approved By / Approuvé par		

B - Buy M - Monitor x - No Further Interest

Date		Stock	Day Hi	Day Low	Day Close	Day Chge	Volume	52-Week Hi	52-Week Low	Previous Week Hi	Previous Week Low	Previous Week Close	Previous Week Chge	Volume	
Oct. 6	B	Teck B wt	1.55	1.20	1.55	+45	21000	20 1/4	0.70	1.25	0.90	1.10	+10	32000	Bought 2000 @ 1.65 500 @ 1.70 Oct. 7
Oct. 11	~~M~~	Renaissance	11 7/8	11 3/8	11 3/4	+3/4	102482	17 7/8	10 1/2	12 1/4	10 1/2	11	-1 5/8	1437000	Making new lows - M +1/2 Oct. 12 inc. Oct. 13 Stabilized 12-13 range X
	~~M~~	Wharf	5	4.50	5	+60	172000	8 7/8	3.25	4.50	4.20	4.40	-10	62000	
	B	Wharf wt	1.95	1.50	1.95	+35	4700	5 3/8	1.10	1.60	1.25	1.60	+25	11000	Watch with → Bought 2000 @ 2.10 Oct. 12
Oct. 12	X	Pacific Transocean	1.05	0.91	1.05	+14	68350	5 1/2	0.91	1.25	1.00	1.00	-17	233000	Hitting new lows X
Oct. 17	X	Goldpost	1.10	0.85	1.10	+25	64862	2.79	0.80	1.05	0.85	0.85	-15	385000	Oct. 18 - No. Vol. - price off X
	X	Treminco	0.75	0.65	0.75	+15	79834	1.40	0.55	0.65	0.55	0.60	-9	16000	Oct. 18 - Vol. Good - price off X
	~~M~~	Twin Res. B	0.77	0.75	0.77	+12	31000	1.40	0.55	0.65	0.55	0.65	+5	159000	Oct. 18 - No Vol. +13 - M
Oct. 18	~~M~~	Counsel wt	0.55	0.27	0.55	+35	17200	2.80	0.04	0.30	0.20	0.22	-8	48000	Oct. 19 - Vol. low - price steady - M
	X	Poco Pete wt	0.75	0.55	0.70	+15	22700	8	0.32	0.50	0.40	0.50	+10	47000	Oct. 19 - Opened Down X
Oct. 19	X	Aber Res.	0.85	0.70	0.85	+25	101347	2.30	0.55	1.05	0.90	0.90	-15	5000	Hit low this week Oct. 20. n.t. B-84 A-90 X
Oct. 19	X	Gemini T	1.39	1.25	1.39	+19	35500	4.00	1.20	1.44	1.30	1.35	-2	26000	Opened Down X
	X	Northwest Digital	1.00	0.85	1.00	+15	21271	2.50	0.70	N/A	N/A	N/A	N/A	N/A	Opened Down X
Oct. 25	X	National Business	1.99	1.71	1.99	+32	268200	17 1/2	1.40	1.72	1.52	1.67	+6	212000	Opened Down X
	~~M~~	Pioneer Metals	3.40	3.10	3.40	+25	587508	12	3.00	3.40	3.00	3.10	-15	200000	No change - M
Oct. 26	~~M~~	Quartz M.	1.10	0.95	1.10	+25	37900	2.95	0.85	1.15	1.02	1.02	-9	43000	Oct. 27 - Opened slightly down - M Oct. 31 - off X
Oct. 28	~~M~~	Euro Nevada	4.00	3.50	4.00	+50	35704	8.00	3.25	3.60	3.45	3.45	-10	61000	Oct. 31 - Opened Even - M
	X	Euro Nevada wt	2.00	1.50	1.95	+55	19304	6 1/4	1.20	1.60	1.40	1.40	-20	71000	
	~~M~~	Noramco	1.38	1.22	1.38	+18	134800	7	1.15	1.62	1.30	1.36	-24	139000	Oct. 31 - Opened Even - M
	~~M~~	Wharf wt	2.15	1.85	2.10	+50	36850	5 5/8	1.10	2.10	1.65	1.70	-40	20000	Oct. 31 - Opened steady - M
Nov. 1	~~M~~	FPI Ltd.	10	9 3/8	9 7/8	+5/8	170490	17 5/8	8	9 3/4	8 3/4	9 1/2	+5/8	593000	Nov. 2 Vol. Down - price even Nov. 3 Price & Vol. off X
	~~M~~	LFP Holdings	0.60	0.50	0.60	+15	37000	1.50	0.35	0.40	0.37	0.40	+2	12000	Nov. 2 - Good price - No. vol - M
Nov. 2	X	Cambior wt	3.60	3.25	3.60	+35	23300	12 1/2	2.75	3.40	3.20	3.25	-15	64000	Opened Down X
	~~M~~	Echo Bay	19 1/2	18 1/2	19 3/8	+7/8	286565	33 7/8	18 1/4	19 1/2	18 3/8	18 3/4	-3/4	560000	No change - M /
	X	Equity Silver	5 1/4	4.75	5 1/4	+45	50600	7 7/8	4.00	4.90	4.70	4.80	-15	95000	Opened Down X
	X	Pegasus	16 1/8	15 5/8	16 1/8	+3/4	43700	26 1/2	11 1/4	15 5/8	15 1/8	15 1/4	-1/4	166000	No change - Low vol. X
Nov. 3	X	Cableshare A	0.60	0.55	0.59	+9	111300	4.20	0.48	0.75	0.66	0.69	-1	23000	Making new lows X
Nov. 7	B	Eastmaque Gold	4.10	3.15	4.10	+95	126100	9 1/2	2.70	3.15	2.95	3.15	+10	112000	Nov. 8 - Bought 1000 @ 4.15
	B M	Petromet Res.	0.80	0.65	0.80	+14	224500	2.10	0.61	0.75	0.65	0.66	-14	30000	Nov. 8 - Opened even - M +7 Nov. 9 Nov. 14 Bought 5000 @ 0.90

B-Buy M-Monitor X - No Further Interest

Date		Stock	Day Hi	Day Low	Day Close	Day Chge	Volume	52-Week Hi	52-Week Low	Previous Week Hi	Previous Week Low	Previous Week Close	Previous Week Chge	Previous Week Volume	Remarks
Nov.8	XM	Goldteck	0.52	0.42	0.50	+10	91500	1.60	0.28	0.43	0.40	0.42	+2	119000	Opened Even - M
	X	Saintilore	3.50	3.00	3.40	+35	68367	8 3/4	2.10	2.70	2.10	2.70	+20	81000	Opened Down X
Nov.10	X	Golden Star	3.10	2.70	3.00	+50	26478	4.70	2.15	2.85	2.45	2.45	-40	44000	Opened Down X
	X	Renaissance	11 5/8	11 1/4	11 1/2	+1/2	36156	17 7/8	10 1/2	12 3/8	11 5/8	11 5/8	-5/8	276000	Opened Down X
Nov.15	XM	Cableshare A	0.70	0.60	0.70	+12	56500	4.20	0.48	0.72	0.60	0.60	-10	156000	Opened Even - M
Nov.17	XM	Linamar Machine	6 5/8	6	6 5/8	+5/8	275410	10 1/4	5 1/2	6 1/4	5 3/4	6	+1/2	26000	Price even - Vol down - M
Nov.22	XM	Plastic Engine	1.20	1.03	1.18	+18	40875	2.00	0.85	1.20	1.00	1.00	-20	111000	Opened even - M
Nov.23	B	Falconbridge wt	2.70	2.40	2.63	+18	51800	3.95	1.20	2.75	2.42	2.47	-15	77000	Bought 1500 @ 2.75 - Nov.24
Nov.24	X	Nuinsco Res.	1.10	0.88	1.08	+13	227600	3.60	0.50	0.85	0.80	0.85	—	7000	Opened Down X
Nov.25	X	Golden Knight wT	1.00	0.80	0.95	+15	29000	3.00	0.79	1.14	0.91	1.19	-24	51000	Opened Down X
Nov.28	XM	Campbell Res.	1.00	0.95	1.00	+12	42075	2.65	0.85	0.98	0.85	0.88	-17	45000	Opened even - M Down Dec.1 X
Nov.29	X	Eco Corp	10 3/4	9 1/2	10 1/2	+1 1/4	35800	18 1/2	5 1/2	10 1/4	8 7/8	9	-3/4	50000	Opened Down - Low vol. X
Dec.1	XM	Fleet Aerospace Ser.1 Pr	4.30	3.90	4.30	+45	22600	6 1/2	3.50	4.00	3.85	4.00	+25	24000	Traded even - M -30 - Dec.5 X
	X	Goldteck	0.48	0.39	0.45	+8	78000	1.60	0.28	0.45	0.37	0.37	-7	163000	Opened Down X
	XM	Nelson Holdings	0.40	0.38	0.39	+8	41000	0.95	0.17	0.28	0.17	0.20	+2	70000	Traded even - M
Dec.2	XM	BYG Natural Trs.	0.83	0.75	0.83	+13	47500	1.59	0.45	0.65	0.60	0.65	—	13000	Traded even - M Dec.8 - No action X
	XM	Hemlo Gold	11 7/8	11 1/8	11 7/8	+7/8	132510	19 3/4	10 3/4	12	11 5/8	11 7/8	+1/4	144000	Traded even - M " " X
	X	Pacific Transocean	0.45	0.33	0.45	+9	114500	4.35	0.33	0.52	0.41	0.48	+4	284000	Making new lows X
	XM	Queenston Gold	2.23	2.10	2.23	+22	71900	3.40	1.15	2.15	1.85	2.05	-5	514000	Low vol. - M Dec.6 - Vol. off - Price off X
Dec.5	B	Ican Minerals	0.52	0.40	0.52	+12	59000	1.20	0.30	0.42	0.40	0.40	-4	98000	Dec.6 - Bought 7000 @ 0.58
Dec.7	X	Doman B	7 1/2	7	7 1/2	+5/8	22800	11 3/4	4.70	7 3/4	6 7/8	7	-7/8	51000	Dec.8 - Price down - no vol. X
Dec.8	X	Compu-Home	0.60	0.52	0.60	+10	59500	1.05	0.21	0.40	0.30	0.40	+3	24000	Opened Down X
Dec.8	X	Plastic Engine	1.14	1.00	1.14	+13	334100	2.00	0.85	1.19	1.13	1.15	—	203000	Opened even - No. Vol. X
Dec.15	B M	Cableshare A	0.62	0.52	0.62	+10	563900	4.20	0.48			N/A			Opened even - M Dec.20 - Bought 5000 @ 0.70
	XM	Highwood	2.40	2.15	2.40	+25	51100	3.85	2.10			N/A			2.50 B - 2.70 A No Trades - M
	XM	Pacific Transocean	0.45	0.40	0.45	+9	59883	4.35	0.33			N/A			Opened even - M Crashed - Dec.21
Dec.16	XM	Inco	29 7/8	27 1/2	29 3/4	+1 3/8	2688260	42 1/2	22 1/8			N/A			Price steady - vol. large - M Moved out of price range.
	XM	Redstone	0.80	0.70	0.78	+12	154100	1.14	0.18			N/A			Vol. & Price steady - M
	B M	Sedona Ind.	1.14	1.10	1.13	+13	33600	1.60	0.95			N/A			Vol. Down - Price steady - M Dec.20 Bought 3000 @ 1.25

Prepared By / Préparé par	Initials / Initiales	Date
Approved By / Approuvé par		

Prepared By / Préparé par	Initials / Initiales	Date
Approved By / Approuvé par		

B-Buy M-Monitor X-No Further Interest

Date		Stock	Day Hi	Day Low	Day Close	Day Chge	Day Volume	52-Week Hi	52-Week Low	Previous Week Hi	Previous Week Low	Previous Week Close	Previous Week Chge	Previous Week Volume	
Dec.19	X	Cnda. Tungsten wt	0.65	0.65	0.65	+12	96000	1.70	0.35	0.53	0.35	0.53	-2	11000	Opened Down X
	X	Excel Energy	0.84	0.75	0.84	+11	713976	1.51	0.56	0.78	0.72	0.73	-2	276000	Opened Down X
	B	New Que Raglan	3.00	2.80	3.00	+25	22200	4.35	1.50	2.75	2.40	2.75	+25	35000	Bought 1500 @ 3.20 - Dec.20
	X	Seabright Expl.	0.70	0.65	0.70	+10	108070	4.50	0.60	0.70	0.60	0.60	-10	5000	Price even - Vol. off X
Dec.20	~~M~~	Canada Northwest	8½	7¾	8½	+⅝	20900	20	6½	7¾	6½	7⅝	+⅝	129000	Opened even - M Dec.22 - price & vol. off X
	X	Eco Corp	10⅜	9½	10¼	+½	23150	18½	5½	9⅝	8¾	9⅜	+⅜	27000	Opened Down X
	~~M~~	Golden Terrace	0.53	0.40	0.50	+8	73500	1.35	0.27	0.38	0.32	0.38	+7	95000	Mixed trading - M Down Dec.22 X
Dec.21	X	Plexus	1.75	1.61	1.75	+20	54600	4.65	1.70	1.80	1.55	1.75	+5	48000	Opened down X
Dec.22	~~M~~	Cont'l Pharma A	0.70	0.60	0.70	+18	86600	3.05	0.52	0.80	0.60	0.60	-30	30000	Price steady - no vol. - M Off - Dec.28 X
	~~M~~	Discrete Time Sys.	0.60	0.55	0.60	+11	23000	0.90	0.44	0.64	0.50	0.55	-6	32000	Price steady - no. vol. - M Price off - Dec.27
	X	Interaction Res.	1.85	1.70	1.85	+24	83400	2.20	1.51	1.70	1.64	1.64	-60	23000	Price off - Vol. Down X
	X	Jascan	0.56	0.48	0.55	+7	118000	0.79	0.38	0.42	0.38	0.42	+2	139000	" " " " X
	M	Polysteel	0.90	0.80	0.90	+18	24000	4.00	0.66	0.85	0.66	0.80	-5	47000	Price steady - vol. down - M Down Jan.3 X
Dec.29	~~M~~	Nexus	0.70	0.67	0.67	+9	21266	1.56	0.44			N/A			Opened even - M No Trades - Jan 5 X
	~~M~~	Socanav wt	0.50	0.45	0.50	+8	39000	1.50	0.25			N/A			Price even - Vol. off - M Jan.6 No action X
	B	Trident	1.60	1.35	1.49	+20	75300	8¾	1.00			N/A			Dec.30 - Bought 3000 @ 1.55
Dec.30	~~M~~	Aur Res	3.45	3.05	3.45	+40	37950	6¾	3.00			N/A			Price even - vol. down - M Vol - Price off Jan.3 X
	~~M~~	Echo Bay	16¾	16⅛	16¾	+⅝	77050	30⅞	15⅝			N/A			Opened even - M Jan.6 - No action X
	X	Golden Shield	0.40	0.35	0.40	+7	66025	1.99	0.30			N/A			Opened down X
1989															
Jan.3	~~M~~	Roddy Res.	0.85	0.80	0.85	+10	22000	2.95	0.55	0.75	0.55	0.75	+5	30000	Opened even - M off - Jan.6 X
Jan.4	~~M~~	Eco Corp	10⅝	9⅞	10⅝	+¾	53610	18½	5½	10	9¾	10	—	2000	Jan.5 - Unable to buy Fully invested - closed up 1⅜
		Fully invested - only tracking for future prospects													
Jan.5	~~M~~	Mitel Corp.	3.30	2.95	3.30	+35	83700	4.40	2.55						Trading even - Jan.6 M Jan.9 - No action X
	~~M~~	Noranda F	15	14¼	15	+⅞	108705	20½	13¼						Trading slightly off - Jan.6 - M Jan.9 - No action X
	X	Rea Gold	3.35	3.10	3.35	+30	61700	4.30	2.30						Closed @ 3.60 - Jan.6 - too high X
	~~M~~	Ventech	1.65	1.30	1.65	+35	28079	3.60	0.90						Jan.6 - Trading slightly up - M
Jan.6	~~M~~	Coxheath Gold	0.70	0.52	0.65	+13	26000	1.70	0.48	0.68	0.62	0.66	+6	23000	Price even - vol. down - M
	~~M~~	Ego Res.	0.72	0.62	0.69	+9	116400	1.55	0.35	0.62	0.60	0.62	-1	20000	" " M

Prepared By / Préparé par	Initials / Initiales	Date
Approved By / Approuvé par		

B - Buy   M - Monitor   X - No Further Interest

Date		Stock	Day Hi	Day Low	Day Close	Day Chge	Volume	52-Week Hi	52-Week Low	Previous Week Hi	Previous Week Low	Previous Week Close	Previous Week Chge	Previous Week Volume	
Jan. 6	X	Plexus	2.10	1.80	2.05	+21	26300	4.65	1.30	1.75	1.65	1.75	+5	13000	Vol. & price down X
Jan. 9	~~M~~	Sceptre Res.	3.55	3.25	3.55	+35	198869	4.90	3.00	3.25	3.15	3.20	—	129000	Opened even - M Jan. 13 - No action X
	B	Lanpar Tech	0.79	0.60	0.79	+11	22500	2.05	0.32	0.70	0.68	0.68	-2	22000	Jan. 10 - Bought 5000 @ 0.84
Jan. 10	~~M~~	Amer. Barrick wt	6 5/8	6	6 5/8	+3/4	90000	9 1/2	5 1/4	6	5 3/4	5 7/8	+3/8	10000	Opened even - M Jan. 13 - No action
Jan. 10	X	Cdn. Natural Res.	0.45	0.30	0.40	+18	471700	0.45	0.10	0.20	0.17	0.17	—	53000	Price down on large vol. X
	~~M~~	Resource Capital	4.50	4.10	4.50	+40	1115100	8	3.75	4.10	4.00	4.00	-5	80000	Price steady - low vol. M
Jan. 11	~~M~~	Int'l Thunderwood	0.70	0.58	0.56	+8	43500	2.20	0.52	0.75	0.54	0.58	-22	103000	Opened even - M
	~~M~~	Syngold Expl.	0.54	0.43	0.54	+8	37950	1.70	0.43	0.63	0.50	0.53	-13	89000	" " - M
Jan. 13	~~M~~	BCED wt	0.65	0.58	0.65	+8	42600	1.24	0.55	0.60	0.50	0.60	+2	19000	Price even - vol. down - M Jan. 17 - no action X
	~~M~~	Golden Rule	2.15	1.80	2.15	+35	18100	4.65	1.55	1.90	1.65	1.80	+6	17000	Vol. up - price even - M Jan. 20 - no action X
Jan. 16	X	Coseka Res.	0.42	0.35	0.40	+6	134200	0.97	0.16	0.35	0.28	0.34	+6	294000	Opened down X
Jan. 17	X	Cambior wt	2.25	2.11	2.25	+17	46450	7 7/8	1.80	2.10	1.80	2.01	-24	141000	Down - Jan. 18 X
	B M	Tee Comm	0.85	0.75	0.85	+12	35000	2.75	0.61	0.80	0.63	0.75	+10	334000	Opened even - M Bought 5000 @ 0.90 Jan. 19
	B	Viceroy Res.	6 1/4	5 7/8	6 1/4	+1 1/8	21650	11	4.00	5	4.40	5	+3/8	169000	Bought 600 @ 6 3/4 - Jan. 18
Jan. 18	~~M~~	Icon Minerals	0.84	0.75	0.80	+12	85000	1.12	0.30	0.94	0.74	0.76	-14	380000	Opened even - M Jan. 23 - no action X
Jan. 19	B	Campbell Res.	1.20	1.10	1.20	+15	63343	2.31	0.75	1.10	0.87	1.10	+25	53000	Bought 3000 @ 1.25 - Jan. 20
	B M	Cambior wt	2.25	2.12	2.25	+14	52350	7 7/8	1.80	2.10	1.80	2.01	-24	141000	Creeping up on volume for 3 days - M Bought 1500 @ 2.45 Jan. 20
	~~M~~	Fahnestock A	2.20	2.03	2.20	+20	19000	3.05	1.60	1.95	1.80	1.95	+15	21000	Opened down Jan. 25 with no action X
	X	Lanpar Tech	1.14	1.00	1.14	+14	21700	2.05	0.32	1.25	0.60	0.82	+14	212000	Opened down X
Jan. 20	B	Aur Res.	3.30	3.05	3.30	+25	38750	6 3/4	2.85	3.15	2.95	3.00	-25	252000	Bought 1500 @ 3.40 - Jan. 23
	X	Breakwater	4.35	4.05	4.35	+35	54290	6 3/8	3.70	4.05	3.75	4.05	+20	91000	No change Jan. 23 X
	B	Equity Silver A	4.45	4.00	4.30	+30	151200	6 7/8	3.80	4.05	3.80	3.80	-25	176000	Bought 1000 @ 4.50 Jan. 23
	X	Glen Auden	0.52	0.45	0.52	+7	82000	1.04	0.38	0.45	0.42	0.45	—	37000	Opened even X
	~~M~~	Lynngold Res.	1.75	1.60	1.75	+25	115100	3.00	1.50	1.60	1.50	1.60	-10	16000	Vol. off - price up slightly - M Jan. 25 No action X
Jan. 20	X	Madeleine Mines	2.90	2.65	2.89	+24	38300	5 3/4	2.01	2.45	2.21	2.32	+9	117000	Price & Vol. off X
	X	Minven Gold	3.60	3.30	3.60	+25	54166	4.86	3.15	3.55	3.15	3.30	-25	97000	No spread X
	X	Northway Expl.	0.70	0.55	0.66	+31	105500	0.95	0.35	0.44	0.44	0.44	-2	5000	No spread X
	~~M~~	Roddy Res.	0.95	0.87	0.95	+12	23400	2.50	0.55	0.95	0.90	0.94	+2	31000	Vol. off - price even - M Jan. 30 - Down X
Jan. 23	~~M~~	Cons. TVX	6 1/2	6 1/8	6 1/2	+7/8	115250	11 3/4	4.70	5 7/8	5 1/8	5 5/8	+5/8	247000	Opened even - M off - Jan. 27 X

RAND & TOY - L16-99084

	Initials / Initiales	Date
Prepared By / Préparé par		
Approved By / Approuvé par		

B-Buy M-Monitor X-No Further Interest

Date		Stock	Day Hi	Day Low	Day Close	Day Chge	Volume	52-Week Hi	52-Week Low	Previous Week Hi	Previous Week Low	Previous Week Close	Previous Week Chge	Volume	
Jan.23	~~M~~	Granges	3.85	3.55	3.85	+30	66211	7½	3.00	3.55	3.25	3.55	+20	286000	Opened even - M off - Jan. 27 X
Jan.25	X	Goldex Mines	1.40	1.24	1.40	+20	28158	3.50	1.20	1.75	1.65	1.65	-10	11000	Price even - vol. off X
	X	Skyline	11	9⅞	11	+⅞	257200	17¾	8	11⅝	10¼	10⅝	-⅝	82000	Opened slightly up - vol. way off X
Jan.26	B	United Reef	0.55	0.43	0.54	+11	273448	1.84	0.33	0.45	0.38	0.42	+3	203000	Bought 6000 @ 0.60 - Jan. 27
Jan.27	~~M~~	Abitibi wt	1.05	0.90	1.03	+14	44500	4.90	0.60	0.82	0.75	0.80	+10	28000	Trading slow - Jan. 30 - M Jan. 31 - no action X
	~~M~~	BCED wt	1.00	0.75	0.82	+18	41550	1.24	0.55	0.65	0.58	0.58	-7	60000	Opened even - M Feb. 1 - off X
	~~M~~	Polysteel	1.30	0.87	1.24	+39	31300	1.00	0.66	0.80	0.75	0.80	—	7000	Opened even - M Feb. 1 - off X
Jan.31	X	Arbor Capital A	6⅛	5½	6⅛	+⅝	20200	11⅜	5	6⅛	6	6⅛	+⅝	17000	Price even - no. vol. X
	~~M~~	Fleet Aero A	1.80	1.75	1.80	+30	30589	1.60	1.50	1.80	1.75	1.75	-5	17000	Feb. 1 1.80 B - 1.85 A - no trades - M Feb. 3 - No action X
	X	Moneta Porcupine	0.70	0.57	0.70	+16	39500	1.20	0.40	0.64	0.50	0.50	-7	57000	Opened even - vol. off X
	B	Scintilore	1.19	0.96	1.17	+25	118115	8¾	0.70	1.95	0.70	0.85	-1.05	726000	Bought 3000 @ 1.20 Feb. 1
	X	Wharf	5¼	4.75	5¼	+50	48800	6⅞	4.15	5¼	4.75	4.75	-25	220000	Not enough spread X

RAND & TOY - L16-99084

RAND & TOY - L16-99084

Transactions

Date 1988	Stock	Bought Price	Bought No. of Shares	Cut Loss	Target	Sold Price	Sold No. of Shares	Profit (Loss)	Date
Sep. 8	Golden Knight wt	2.30	2000	2.00	3.70	1.95	2000	(0.35)	Sep. 12
Sep. 8	SHL Systemhouse	9.00	500	8.00	32.00	10 3/4	500	1 3/4	Sep. 20
Sep. 22	Granges	3.85	1000	3.45	15 7/8	3.90	1000	0.05	Oct. 11
Sep. 28	Ego Res.	0.57	7000	0.50	2.70	1.04	7000	0.47	Nov. 9
Sep. 30	Polysteel	1.10	3500	0.90	6.00	1.25	3500	0.15	Oct. 7
Oct. 4	Falconbridge	21 1/2	200	19 1/2	30 3/4	23	200	1 1/2	Nov. 4
Oct. 5	Golden Rule	2.00	2000	1.75	8 5/8	1.95	2000	(0.05)	Oct. 17
Oct. 7	Teck B wt	1.80	2000	1.60	20.00	2.40	2000	0.60	Oct. 19
Oct. 12	Wharf wt	2.10	2000	1.85	5 7/8	1.95	2000	(0.15)	Oct. 19
Nov. 8	Eastmaque Gold	4.15	1000	3.75	9 1/2	3.95	1000	(0.20)	Dec. 8
Nov. 16	Petromet	0.90	5000	0.80	2.10	1.50	5000	0.60	Dec. 6
Nov. 24	Falconbridge wt	2.75	1500	2.45	3.95	6 1/2	1500	3.75	Jan. 23
Dec. 6	Ican Minerals	0.58	7000	0.50	1.20	0.90	7000	0.32	Jan. 6
Dec. 20	Cableshare A	0.70	5000	0.60	4.20	0.80	5000	0.10	Jan. 9
Dec. 20	Sedona Ind.	1.25	3000	1.10	1.60	1.90	3000	0.65	Jan. 31
Dec. 20	New Que. Raglan	3.20	1500	2.85	4.35	4.60	1500	1.40	Jan. 4
Dec. 30	Tridont	1.55	3000	1.35	8 5/8	1.65	3000	0.10	Jan. 6

Transactions cont'd

Date 1989	Stock	Bought Price	Bought No. of Shares	Cut Loss	Target	Sold Price	Sold No. of Shares	Profit (Loss)	Date
Jan.10	Langar Tech.	2.34	5000	0.70	2.05	1.10	5000	0.26	Jan.12
Jan.17	Viceroy Res.	6¼	600	6.00	11	6.00	600	(¾)	Jan.30
Jan.19	Tee Comm.	0.90	5000	0.78	2.75	0.82	5000	(0.08)	Jan.31
Jan.20	Campbell Res.	1.25	3000	1.05	2.31	1.05	3000	(0.20)	Jan.30
Jan.20	CamBior wt	2.45	1500	2.20	7¼	2.80	1500	(0.35)	Jan.27
Jan.23	Aur Res.	3.40	1500	3.00	6¾	3.25	1500	(0.15)	Jan.27
Jan.23	Equity Silver A	4.50	1000	4.00	6⅛	4.00	1000	(0.50)	Jan.27
Jan.27	United Reef	0.60	6000	0.50	1.89	0.50	6000	(0.10)	Jan.30

Account Summary

Opening Balance – $20,000   C – Transaction Closed

Date 1988	Stock		Bought Price	Bought No. of Shares	Sold Price	Sold No. of Shares	Commiss.	Total	Balance
Sep. 8	Golden Knight wt	C	2.30	2000			138 –	4738 –	15262 –
Sep. 8	SHL Systemhouse	C	9.00	500			135 –	4635 –	10627 –
Sep.12	Golden Knight wt	C			1.95	2000	58 50	3841 50	14468 50
Sep.20	SHL Systemhouse	C			10¾	500	80 63	5294 37	19762 87
Sep.22	Granges	C	3.85	1000			115 50	3965 50	15797 37
Sep.28	Ego Res.	C	0.57	7000			119 70	4109 70	11687 67
Sep.30	Polysteel	C	1.10	3500			115 50	3965 50	7722 17
Oct. 4	Falconbridge	C	21½	200			129 –	4429 –	3293 17
Oct. 5	Golden Rule	C	2.00	2000			120 –	4120 –	(826 83)
Oct. 7	Polysteel	C			1.25	3500	65 63	4309 37	3482 54
Oct. 7	Teck B wt	C	1.80	2000			108 –	3708 –	(225 46)
Oct. 11	Granges	C			3.90	1000	58 50	3841 50	3616 04
Oct. 12	Wharf wt	C	2.10	2000			126 –	4326 –	(709 96)
Oct. 17	Golden Rule	C			1.95	2000	58 50	3841 50	3131 54
Oct. 19	Teck B wt	C			2.40	2000	72 –	4728 –	7959 54
Oct. 19	Wharf wt	C			1.95	2000	58 50	3841 50	11701 04
Nov. 4	Falconbridge	C			23.00	200	69 00	4531 –	16232 04
Nov. 8	Eastmague Gold	C	9.15	1000			124 50	4274 50	11957 54

Account Summary cont'd.

Date 1988	Stock		Bought Price	No. of Shares	Sold Price	No. of Shares	Commiss.	Total	Balance
Nov.9	Ego Res.	C			1.09	7000	218.40	7061.60	19019.14
Nov.16	Petromet	C	0.90	5000			135 –	4635 –	14384.14
Nov.24	Falconbridge wt	C	2.75	1500			123.75	4248.75	10135.39
Dec.6	Petromet	C			1.50	5000	112.50	7387.50	17522.89
Dec.6	Ican Minerals	C	0.58	7000			121.80	4181.80	13341.09
Dec.8	Eastmague Gold	C			3.95	1000	59.25	3890.75	17231.84
Dec.20	Cableshare A	C	0.70	5000			105 –	3605 –	13626.84
Dec.20	Sedona Ind.	C	1.25	3000			112.50	3862.50	9764.34
Dec.20	New Que. Raglan	C	3.20	1500			144 –	4944 –	4820.34
Dec.30	Trident	C	1.55	3000			139.50	4789.50	30.84
1989									
Jan.A	New Que Raglan	C			4.60	1500	103.50	6796.50	6827.34
Jan.6	Trident	C			1.65	3000	74.25	4875.75	11703.09
Jan.6	Ican Minerals	C			0.90	7000	99.50	6205.50	17908.59
Jan.9	Cableshare A	C			0.80	5000	60 –	3940 –	21848.59
Jan.10	Lonpar Tech	C	0.84	5000			126 –	4326 –	17522.59
Jan.12	Lonpar Tech	C			1.10	5000	82.50	5417.50	22940.09
Jan.17	Viceroy Res	C	6¾	600			121.50	4171.50	18768.59

Account Summary cont'd

Date 1989	Stock		Bought Price	Bought No. of Shares	Sold Price	Sold No. of Shares	Commiss.	Total	Balance
Jan. 19	Tee Comm.	c	0.90	5000			135 -	4635 -	1413359
Jan. 20	Campbell Res.	c	1.25	3000			112 50	386250	1027109
Jan. 20	Cambior wt	c	2.45	1500			110 25	378525	648584
Jan. 23	Falconbridge wt	c			6½	1500	292 50	9457 50	1594334
Jan. 23	Aur Res.	c	3.40	1500			153 -	5253 -	1069034
Jan. 23	Equity Silver A	c	4.50	1000			135 -	4635 -	605534
Jan. 27	Cambior wt	c			2.80	1500	63 -	4137 -	1019234
Jan. 27	Aur Res.	c			3.25	1500	73 13	480187	1499421
Jan. 27	Equity Silver A	c			4.00	1000	60 -	3940 -	1893421
Jan. 27	United Reef	c	0.60	6000			108 -	3708 -	1522621
Jan. 30	Viceroy Res.	c			6.00	600	55 -	3545 -	1877121
Jan. 30	Campbell Res.	c			1.05	3000	55 -	3095 -	2186621
Jan. 30	United Reef	c			0.50	6000	55 -	2945 -	2481121
Jan. 31	Sedona Ind.	c			1.90	3000	171 -	5529 -	3034021
Jan. 31	Tee Comm.	c			0.82	5000	61 50	403850	3437871